THE HERMIT
Gabriel D. Roberts

The Hermit

GABRIEL D. ROBERTS

RUBEDO PRESS
AUCKLAND · SEATTLE
2015

© Gabriel D. Roberts 2015

All rights reserved. No part of this work may be reproduced without express permission from the publisher. Brief passages may be cited according to fair use, by way of criticism, scholarship, or review, as long as full acknowledgement is given to the author and the publisher.

This work contains citations from the *I Ching* (trans. Hilary Barrett, *I Ching: Walking your Path; Creating your Future*, London: Arcturus, 2010), and *The Tibetan Book of the Dead: The Great Liberation through Hearing in the Bardo* (trans. by Francesca Fremantle and Chogyam Trungpa, Boston: Shambhala, 2000).

The Hermit
By Gabriel D. Roberts

First edition

Published by Rubedo Press
www.rubedo.press
733 7th Ave, #107
Kirkland, WA 98033, USA

ISBN: 978-1-943710-02-7

Cover photography
by Sam Kiyoumarsi

Design and typography
by Aaron Cheak

*To the explorers of the great mysteries,
be brave, be reckless.*

Contents

Prelude — 13

PART I
Treading in confusion — 19

PART II
Beating a pot and singing — 67

PART III
Clear golden light — 139

PART IV
Sudden it comes — 185

PART V
Tears like flowing streams — 243

PART VI
The king marches out — 327

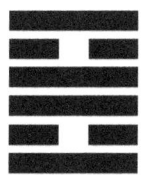

*A hero ventures forth from the world of common day
into a region of supernatural wonder: fabulous forces
are there encountered and a decisive victory is won:
the hero comes back from this mysterious adventure
with the power to bestow boons on his fellow man.*

JOSEPH CAMPBELL
The Hero with a Thousand Faces

Prelude

DEPRESSION IS A DEEP, DARK WELL WHOSE bucket and rope have long since rotten and fallen into its untold depths. The view from the murky depths up into the daylight mocks hope, for the only reality within grasp is the cold-wet stone of the present. It is with eyes full of water from this well that I see these moments past, and from its morose depths draw my words. Though I am now basking in the golden light of a time of harvest, I summon the reflection of those moments in the deepest, darkest corners of my being, because the story I tell is more than mine, it is yours too. As for then, it was the coldest, and though basked in the Southern California sun, it was the blackest. It was from this dark well that I saw and spoke as I stood before my wife and told her, to her white-hot surprise, that our marriage was over.

Our relationship was marked by my attempts to American Dream my way out of the constant feeling that deep down, I was a phony and a failure. It was a kind of slow steady ache that rots like a tooth and never lets you be at ease. Betty had in so many ways been the recipient, accomplice, and victim of my most grand attempts to somehow outdo my unconsciously enslaving drive to be perfect. I leveraged it all a few years prior to move us to New York City to escape a numb reality that I couldn't buy or overwork my way out of. This, my primordial guilt, was a big hurt placed like a poison emerald in my heart, calcified and vulcanized by the voices of my childhood that filled me with a maladjusted sense of worth.

I was once a big shot private jet broker in New York, working from a high rise in Manhattan just past 53rd, a few blocks from the United Nations building. I tried to look like hot shit, but I felt the void of existence lurking all around me. I could not insulate myself from it with my business suit, I could not drown it with whiskey, and could not fuck it out of me; I could only ache for a voice that I had lost all hope of ever hearing. I was withering in the real world where the only real value came from money, and miracles only happen to fools. But then a prophecy came to me one fortuitous day when I found myself in my Queens apartment sinking into the ground, down into the earth, sent there by the consumption of five dried grams of psychedelic mushrooms. There in the dark of the earth, a quiet and lovely feminine creature made from a myriad of beings called to me, beckoning me. "Come to the desert, we will meet you there. Come to the wilderness and we will take care of you". Though I was clean-shaven at the time,

Prelude

she showed me myself as I would later be: with a big beard, washing myself in a mountain stream, drinking from it, bathing in it, restoring an aspect of my primal nature, discovering something I could not find in the city, the arms of a woman, the trappings of a big fancy job, modern distraction, or any other form of satiation.

It was long ago now that this call to the wilderness came; yet it is common among the shamans and the mystics around the world to travel to the wild places, to be alone and suffer the cold and lonesome desolation of the body and the soul. I began this journey like the Fool of the tarot and I fancied that I would spend forty days in the wilderness and return as some transfigured sage who had cloistered himself away from the wicked world and all of its distractions, unstained and miraculous. The reality was to be so different and much more human, full of hardship, loss, loneliness and darkness, the devil's night, the cold and the wet, the agony and the nightmares. But only those who can make it through the void of that lonely night get to glimpse that very first sliver of light in all the wondrous shades of pink, purple, red, and violet. Only those who have tasted the poison and survived know how to turn it into a gift. Victory can be found in the many deaths we see in life and light will be our reward, but that is not where we start this story; we start in the dark.

Treading in confusion.
Honor it, not a mistake.

I CHING, HEXAGRAM 30, LINE I

Chapter 1

AFTER MONTHS OF TURMOIL BETWEEN US two previous splits and recouplings, bouts of counseling, and repeated slides back into the same regurgitated arguments, I was ready either to die or to leave the situation with Betty for good. Six years of countless adventures, struggles, and conflicts all culminated into this one moment. It wasn't something I had ever intended, but it seemed more like we were in each other's way than helping each other along. It had become painfully clear that she was unable, or unwilling to go where I was heading next; too frozen in fear of the present to see into the future. And this wall of ice between us kept us from seeing eye to eye. What had worked before did not work now and what she thought had value had no value to me at all. I felt pinned like a bug under a rock and so I did what I knew best to console myself; I drank her out of my mind night after night and collapsed into our shared marital bed. She disappeared from me like vapor from a boiling pot. When the time came for me to leave I tried to be straightforward and free of insult or injury, but what can really be done in a situation like this? I told it like it was and left it at that. No time to argue, no chance to hear a plea, for all of that had passed, been fucked away, been talked out and ignored. The need to split cut through me like razor wire. For weeks and weeks I'd have panic attacks in the middle of the night and there was no amount of drink that would quiet the cackling voice within me, mocking my futility and powerlessness. Betty and I had become bloated cartoons of our destined selves, too painfully codependent to know it and too far gone to change it. We were a handful of marital clichés made into a greasy sandwich with extra shame-mayo and I couldn't stomach it any longer.

For the first time in my adult life, I had decided to venture out truly on my own and feel what I would soon find as the sting of solitude and poverty. I took four bags and my vintage typewriter, which was my most prized possession, and drove my car to a friend's house where I could prepare for my journey. As I pulled away, Betty just stood there in shock, like a child whose balloon had just burst. "You can't do this, I can't believe you are doing this", but what was so unbelievable about it? I had been unemployed for a solid six months by this time and she daily bore down on me about it. Los Angeles is not New York, the options are fewer and further between, and the roads to each possibility are miles apart. Not a weekend earlier, she spent two hours telling me what a failure

Treading in Confusion

I had become: "I have respectable friends in science, friends that are doctors, I want to get back to school and become a doctor too", I cried. "Your friends live in their grandparents basements with their doctorates", she retorted. She insisted that we must pay off our thousands of dollars of debt by working some kind of corporate job and then, maybe after a couple years of that, I could return to graduate school. That put my mind in a black hole where no future with Betty looked remotely possible, or remotely happy, so when I piled into that car, I drove away with the relief one feels when they have finally vomited after a day-long rampup; the spittle pooling and the rocks in the stomach brewing up like a percolator. I knew that a shit storm would ensue, that hearts would break and that I would be jumping once again into an abyss of sorts. But this wasn't like the last time I had faced a new epoch in my life. I had married before and my marriage to Betty was to be my answer to the mistakes of the first. Last time it was dirty in all the wrong ways, an attempt to salvage 27 years of religious lies and what I thought to be lifelong friends turned fair weather. This time it was about making calculated decisions, to leverage all I had worked for in order to gain all I desired.

Up to this point, Los Angeles had been a bust, no jobs big or small, no trains, lots of fuel costs, six months of bad times. I spent month upon months applying for jobs I knew I would not be able to stand, to pay for shit I didn't want. I knew the dam would burst, but I had no idea where the flood would wash me out. When I left, I did so with a single-minded goal, to make enough money to push the reset button on my life and to make my forty day journey of transformation. After getting to a safe place with my friends, Albert and Macy, I began to plan for my trip up north to trim weed. I had heard there was a green gold rush and with the right connections, one could have enough to change direction. This was the perfect remedy for my total financial drought. That wasn't to say there wasn't a decent amount of peril involved. Humboldt County was hundreds of miles away and I was soon to give my car back to my freshly jilted ex. Once I got there, there would be no guarantee that work would materialize immediately. There were rumors of methamphetamine-fueled tweakers with AK47s and boobie-trapped farms. You had to pack light and live out of a tent; so swamp ass, dirty socks and sketchy meal situations all would be par for the course.

I began to plan my trip for the gold rush. The first order of business was to cash out my old 401 K from one of my corporate jobs. A thousand dollars seemed like an amount that could do the trick. I picked up a two-person tent, a large brown backpack, a warm sleeping bag and a few other essentials. I paid my insurance and credit card bills so I could have a little room to breathe. The biggest question was still the issue of transportation. I had considered flying to San Francisco and taking

Treading in Confusion

a bus up to Arcata, but if anything went wrong, or I needed to relocate, I would be at the mercy of a possibly cruel fate now that autumn was upon me. Instead I opted to throw a Hail Mary and leverage all of my credit for a new phone account and a new vehicle. But this was a tight budget and any exorbitant expenses could prematurely sink this venture. No, I needed something perfect for the job and I knew just the thing.

I walked into Del Rio Motorsports and ran my credit for zero down on a new motorcycle. Only one creditor came back with approval. Yamaha was running a special rebate deal, which worked as a down payment. I was in, but I had to decide which bike would be ideal for me. Being a resident of LA and planning to start grad school in January, I needed something that would kick ass on the freeway and turn heads if I ever wanted to impress a girl. It came down to one perfect selection, the 2013 Yamaha R6. The R6 was an impressive vehicle weighing 413 pounds wet, 110 horsepower and forty miles per gallon. It seemed a clear boon for my endeavors to come across a deal like this—one which afforded me a month to come up with the cash that I didn't presently have to pay for this fuel injected Gnostic missile.

The next order of business was to get insured. Luckily, my insurance company told me that I would be covered for liability on the bike until I could find proper full coverage. The only thing that loomed in my mind was that I couldn't crash and have it be my fault! Now that I was in the safe zone, I was able to drop off the car that my lady and I had shared. I gifted it to her for free, a small peace offering to ensure that we could someday be friends. Now I had wheels, a couple hundred bucks for gas and food, and a means to get up north. Nobody really tells you how painful it can be riding a sport bike intended for the racetrack for seven hours per day. That finely tuned suspension is intended to tear holes in the space-time continuum, but isn't very forgiving on I-5 at ninety miles per hour.

The kind of pain in store for an unfortunate rider carrying a forty-pound backpack full of all his earthly belongings is monumental. Such a rider is in for the following: leg cramps from squatting and lifting yourself off the bike to get a little air to your groin, extreme pain like Mike Tyson was using your taint as a punching bag, neck cramps from holding up the bag and shifting head position in order to change lanes safely. All together these issues made me feel like a gigantic cramp on two wheels, the kind of pain that would make Dick Cheney envious to emulate in his terror inquisitions. But the fact was it was this or nothing, and like Bobby Dylan said, "when you've got nothing, you've got nothing to lose".

My first hour on the road was spent dealing with LA stop and go traffic that was to be followed by the bumpiest piece of shit stretch of highway that I-5 had to offer. I was already in a great deal

Treading in Confusion

of pain. I resolved to do my best to make the pain into some kind of yogic exercise, a meditation and a chance to learn what my body was really capable of. That didn't last long and I had to stop. At the rest stop I decided to ditch a few items, which were making the ride unbearable. Several shirts went in the trash along with a 1.5 liter bottle of water. I moved my backpack and my tent to the tail of the R6. This made a world of difference in regard to my basic comfort. While at rest I decided to mount my video camera to the front of my bike where I had setup a mount. I pressed record and headed out.

As I hit the highway, the R6 roared to life like a demon on fire, screaming for vengeance. As she came to speed I settled into the saddle for the next 60–80 mile stretch before the pain again would be unbearable. About two miles up the road I noticed that the camera was no longer there, having doubtlessly leapt off the bike so quickly that I didn't even see it go. It was the first casualty of my voyage and one of the nicer things that I owned. I resolved not to get upset about it, as I had already let go of many valuable things; it was part of the ongoing catharsis. When you are traveling at 80 miles per hour, you would think you would be the fastest dude on the highway, but this is California and I was being passed like I was standing still. I decided that I would ghost behind large trucks that were speeding so that the state patrol would clock them and not me, a plan that seemed to work well and provide me with a slipstream that made wind vibration a little less jarring.

There's something that happens when you are on a motorcycle that a car cannot reveal, you are forced to perceive more, or die. The highway begins to look like a fast moving concrete stream, the glints of sunlight bounce off everything without the protection of tinted windows. Even the wind seems to play with you, like it's in some kind of wrestling match, tugging you a bit to the left, then the right, then the left again. No matter what was going on, you were in some kind of time warp in which all is moving, yet all is still. Underneath you, the race-proven, nimble monster snatches up the miles like the birds of prey hovering overhead snatch up vermin. It is one of the greatest feelings in the world.

With the flick of the wrist, the fly-by-wire throttle takes you from seventy-two to ninety so fast that the world begins to streak faster than your vision can keep up. You can spring to safety, switch lanes and break with an equally frightening quickness. My thoughts danced between my pains, my love for the bike, and my hopes for what that far off place offered to help me once again reinvent my world. I took a stop to stretch at a vantage point and gazed at the long and winding California Aqueduct that meandered some 280 miles along the freeway. Having just come back from a trip to Italy and seeing the water fountains everywhere there, knowing that they ran from the

Treading in Confusion

original Roman water sources made me a bit jaded to this Californian engineering marvel.

As I drew further north, the scenery began to change from dusty desert to rolling hills of grassland. Massive windmills dotted the landscape as I shot up and down the hills and valleys of the highway. The GPS on my phone instructed me through my headphones where to go and when to turn off. I listened to The Clash at full volume, which at freeway speed was barely audible in contrast to the road noise, but "London Calling" never sounded so good. My destination for the day was Berkeley where I would meet up with a friend of a friend. I had never met Suze, but she was kind enough to open up her home and that was all I needed. Exhausted from the first day's ride, I spent a little time on the couch looking at my smartphone beside Suze before laying down on the makeshift bed she provided in the guest room. I slept well.

I woke up early in the morning and decided to pay a surprise visit to a friend who lived in Oakland. Peacock was a very artsy girl, who despite her hippie leanings despised Burning Man culture, primarily because she believed rightly that artists should get paid for their art rather than just giving it away and living in abject poverty. I made it to Peacock's warehouse and had a coffee. We talked about what it would be like up north, how to trim the buds of weed and how to get on the good side of the weed farmers. She fixed me up a couple of boiled eggs, which were much appreciated since I had already run deathly low on cash. That meal sustained me for many hours as I blasted up the majestic 101. Crossing out of Berkeley and over the bridge, the marine layer peeled off to reveal a breathtaking view of the bay with its big ships. The air felt so crisp and clean without being overly cold. I knew today's ride would be better than the previous.

About halfway to Humboldt County I stopped for lunch at a Taco Bell. I normally avoid fast food, but my budget afforded me little space for being a stickler about my diet. I checked my messages from friends who all claimed to know people I could work for, but nothing had come through yet. I was truly flying blind into the arms of chaos. Though I have come to love Eris, the Greek goddess of chaos, she had something less pleasant for me in the law of sowing and reaping. I had sown the seeds of Taco Bell and now was reaping explosive diarrhea. Unfortunately the long stretches of the 101 are without many rest stops or gas stations, so I would hold and hold until my eyeballs would sweat with the desperate need to shit. I finally found a spot only to need to go again just a few miles down the road. Fuck Taco Bell.

By the time I had made my way up to Arcata, the light of day was already beginning to wane. I needed to find a place to set up camp. I was told that the Trinidad State Park had a free place you could camp, so I headed there. I had assumed that there would be dozens of migrant worker types up

Treading in Confusion

there who were looking for work in the weed business, and was surprised to find that I was the only person there at all. Now that it was dark I had to set up my little two-person tent that I had never previously used. With a small flashlight in my mouth I slowly made sense of the jumble of fabric. I pointed the opening of my tent to face the R6 so that I could easily stab anyone who might try to steal it to death. Once I had the tent set up, I threw all of my gear inside and organized my belongings. Now that I was all cozy inside this fabric womb in the heart of a cold, dark forest, I realized that this was the first time in my life that I was truly alone.

I was alone in the sense that I had no companion beside me, no actual residence, no tangible promise of work; it was just my thoughts, my smartphone, and I. I just laid there staring up at the blue walls of the tent, thinking about everything that had already happened up to this point: the chance meetings, the odd situations and coincidences that popped up along the way like little road signs. I looked at the time. It was only eight PM and I was very tired. I opted to stay up until ten so that I wouldn't be up at four AM. I took two large hits of my medical grade, state-approved legal weed, "Tahoe Dreams", and fell into a deep sleep.

Chapter 2

WHEN I AWOKE IN THE MIDDLE OF THE NIGHT to pee, I unzipped my tent and stepped out to a dazzling night sky. I shone my flashlight in all directions out of paranoia and then had a pee. I crawled back in to my tiny tent and wrapped myself back up in my sleeping bag, struggling against the hard ground. To be honest, I had fallen into the sad trap of fat and lazy complacency through the process of marital domestication, having lost my ability to deal with a less than perfect bed, but now was time to toughen up, to stop being such a fucking whiner and live like people had lived for æons prior. I was already learning a lesson about loneliness, a path I had willfully chosen. I dozed off into the morning light and found that the whole tent was soaked in the morning dew. The tent was not actually waterproof and all of my stuff was covered with great drops of water. I wrapped everything up as well as I could and headed back into Arcata, about twelve miles south.

I decided that even though my budget was low, it would be wise to have a proper breakfast, so I stopped in at Luke's Joint, just across from the square where all of the other miscreants and vagabonds had congregated. I didn't look like it from my nicely trimmed beard and my black sweater, but I was one of them now. I sat down and ordered a coffee and a breakfast sandwich and pulled out my Klimt tarot deck. The cards read out: New Adventures, New Love, Friends Breaking Promises, and Success on the Way.

Luke's joint was on the corner of the town square and had an agreeable vibe to it. It felt half like a coffee shop and half like a greasy spoon; the Arcata version of what you might find in the Williamsberg area of Brooklyn. For these reasons, it felt like the most natural place for me in the little town that was otherwise completely foreign to me. As I settled in at my table, A group of visibly roadworn young vagrants sat down beside me. Feeling desperately in need of communication, I offered to read their cards. Each of them seemed very excited to get a tarot reading and one by one got their message. To my shock and surprise, they all said my readings were the most "right on" of any they had ever seen. They offered for me to join them at their table. Baby Jesus, who introduced himself first, was a longhaired and ruddy dude who wore a torn yellow cowboy jacket, the kind with the long tassels. Firefly was an azure-eyed poet from Boulder who wished "to go back in time and be Jack

Keroac's lover". The bespectacled girl was Pinky and I gave her what seemed the shittiest reading, but apparently it was exactly what she needed to hear. I told her it was time for her to stop relying on other people to fix her problems, that the universe was kindly telling her it was time to grow up a bit.

Hampton was a part-time vagrant who looked like a young and dirty, dark-haired James Dean with his bedraggled yet coiffed hair, and eyes hidden behind knockoff Ray Bans. Ben was a full time tramp who simply wanted to travel and see where the road took him. He told me that sitting still wasn't something he ever wanted, that the road was his home. Despite Ben's full-time traveler status, he still had a smart phone and plenty of connections. His promise to help me find work gave me some reassurance since both my cards and my cell phone's lack of messages both foretold of the failure of my friends to generate any work for me. We sat for hours talking about consciousness and psychedelics and weed. They all seemed to like me despite my ghost white beard telling them I was a good decade older than them.

"You're a part of our crew now Gabriel", Baby Jesus said; "We'll make sure you work with us on this next round". It was nice to know my skills of making friends could come in handy exactly when I needed them to. I hung out at the square with all of them and tried my best not to think about looming bills, or the last few dollars I had left that had to last for some unknown amount of time. Once again, night began to fall and I was the only one in the crew who was not flush with cash. The others had just come back from a trim job and had plenty to spend. I chose to drive back to Trinidad Park to set up camp for a second night in a row. Just like the night before, I was totally alone and had now resolved that this would be my home until work could be found. Night fell again and the sting of loneliness surged more deeply into my heart than the night before. I thought of whom I could call, what I would say, how I could connect without sounding too desperate. I called my kids and left a message, "Hi guys, this is daddy, I just wanted to call and say hi. I'm out camping right now and wanted to tell you I miss you and love you". I hung up the phone and tried not to cry for loneliness. Like the night before, I took two hits of Tahoe and closed my eyes.

As dawn broke, I loaded everything back up and instinctually made my way to the place that had been my only comfort, Luke's Joint. With twelve of my last thirty dollars I ordered a coffee and a breakfast. I stared across the street at the town square at all of the leathers and burners and gutter punks, knowing I would be there soon. I milked my coffee for as many hours as I could before I had to step out of the café and hang out at the park. As the hours passed, I felt increasingly uneasy and unsure. It wasn't shame of having to hang out like a migrant worker, but the fear of 'what if' that

Treading in Confusion

loomed in my mind. What if this was a bad idea, what if I couldn't find work, what if I wasn't burner enough, punk enough, or young enough? What if I go without food for the rest of the day? These were all real questions that had no immediate answer.

I sat in the park like the rest of the travelers, awaiting some unknown employer like some kind of wavy-gravied home depot day laborer. A guy named Pilgrim sat down beside me. Pilgrim was like a blonde Bob Marley with long perfect dreads, a skintight button-up shirt, and coral red pants. His fingernails were long and full of grime, something I noticed because I had done my best to keep myself sanitary-looking. He had been playing the banjo the day before and brought it with him wherever he went. He took a look at my new smartphone and ran his dingy claws across its pristine surface, showing me where we were and where in the hills many of the farms were. He handed my phone back and provided me with some keys to finding work. "I think it's too saturated with workers around here. It might be better to go up into the hills where the growers actually are". We exchanged phone numbers and promised to send word if we found work.

Four PM came around and the whole community gathered together and made a communal vegan dinner. People talk about how hypocritical and shitty hippie types can be, but I don't know what they would have said had they been part of that meal. Afterward everyone literally held hands and did an impromptu standing meditation session. I was still too shy and clean cut to feel like participating, but it was only my pride that kept me, not the good grace of my fellow travelers. I checked my phone incessantly hoping for some kind of message, some good news that would get me through the agony and anxiety of being nowhere doing nothing, but nothing came. I stayed in the park until the sun almost set and made my way back to my campsite.

I had finally learned my lesson and ran my tarp over the tent itself. The weather forecast predicted sunny weather for days, so my primary concern was to keep the dew off the tent, so I wouldn't get soaked again. It seemed like I was getting better at this already. For dinner I pulled out a quarter of a baguette that was leftover from lunch. I had eaten the other three quarters of the baguette then. The next day was to be even more of a challenge than the days prior, because I had just put the last of my money into my gas tank. That meant I had no money for food, but enough gas to take me 122 miles. The real question was what to do with that gas. Should I wait around for a third consecutive day for my friends to come through, or should I chance it up in the mountain towns hoping to score work? It was a difficult decision that I opted to tackle the next morning.

Having charged my beat up old laptop at Luke's Joint, I used the power to charge my phone, which I had run down to ten percent during the day. I

Treading in Confusion

played some music to help stave off the sensation of being alone in the pitch-black forest once again. Chelsea Wolfe's voice ran over me like a light dream one has while falling asleep at the beach under shade. I couldn't help but feel like the universe had me right where I was supposed to be even though this didn't feel at all like something 'wonderful'. I suppose that is part of the lesson, that wonderful is not always the plan. Perhaps this is the reminder that though I'm cold, alone, and without cash, I'm still not dead in a ditch, a victim of murder, a child soldier, or a forced laborer in some third world country. Maybe the lesson is that I'm a spoiled fucking brat who fancies himself as some kind of deep philosopher who muses about the loftier considerations of consciousness while the world burns. I begged for this lesson, I longed for it and now that it has come my way, I only wished to say, "take this cup from me if there be another way". It was then that I thought back to my days as a private jet broker. I could hear the voice of my boss as he bellowed across the Manhattan high-rise office, "Gabe, did you close that Embraer deal yet? You gotta get those fuckin' planes flying. How many people have you called today?" "I closed the deal, but the client says he might want to change the date". "Change the date? Did he sign the contract for tomorrow's flight? He did, right? If he did, then he either flies or pays us the twenty-five grand. If he doesn't like it, then fuck'em. That's why we have them sign these contracts". I remembered the office with its veneer of professionalism, ad-banners, men and women in expensive suits talking to their Manhattan clients who were taking helicopters to the Hamptons, eight-passenger jets to the Bahamas, and G5s to Europe. It was exactly like Wall Street, and for good reason. The founders of the brokerage used to be stock brokers and they had brought their model of ruthless money-grubbing to the private jet scene, gleaning the leftovers from the bigger companies, picking off bottom of the barrel customers who flew first class on the airlines and thought maybe they had a little extra to fly private. One guy grabbed asses of the girls in skirts, spat on the floor, and used racial slurs constantly. The environment was disgusting and I had somehow thought that making money here was going to give me pride and status among the wealthy elite of New York. Instead, I was disgusted with myself. Back in the tent I fell asleep about as far away from the noise of New York as I could be, surrounded by the whoosh of wind in the Northern California redwoods.

Chapter 3

MORNING CAME ONCE AGAIN WITH A sobering view of the situation: four dollars and eighty cents in my checking account. Two dollars and ninety-eight cents left on my credit card. The day's plan was decided; I would go into town, buy a cup of coffee, and drink and write and check my messages until I wore out my welcome. This would give me the time I needed to charge my laptop, which in turn would end up charging my phone at night. My good friends, Albert and Macy, were kind enough to wire me some money, but it was not due to come for a couple of days. Even if work didn't come, my hunger would, and I needed to have a game plan.

As I packed up my campsite in preparation for heading to town, an elderly sheriff showed up in his cop car and rolled down the window. "You know, I'm not sure you are allowed to camp here, but it's up to the park ranger to decide". I told him I had been there for a couple of days and saw the ranger the other day, but he hadn't said anything.

"Well, I guess it might be okay, but could you be sure to clean up after yourself? Is that your champagne bottle over there?" No, Sir, I don't drink (or at least I hadn't since my journey began), but I'll be happy to clean it up for you. "Thank you kindly, son. Well, I see you're traveling light. That's a beautiful motorcycle you've got there. I used to come up here camping with nothing but a sleeping bag and a canvas strapped to the back of my old Triumph. There are some roads up here in the hidden parts that are just beautiful, God's country, only accessible by bike. You really should do some exploring". Well sir, I think I'll be sticking around looking for work. The sheriff continued on about his golden days of motorcycles. "I didn't have all that fancy gear you've got. That bike had a six-gallon tank, but I have no idea why they would have done that. I don't know how anybody's kidneys could handle six-gallons of riding on that thing". I laughed respectfully, trying to make use of my white beard and its respectability factor with the elders. "You know I told my wife down in San Francisco how beautiful it was up here and that I wanted to transfer. She said to me 'well you can transfer anywhere you want, just sign these divorce papers'. I think she was trying to tell me something!" He gave me a wink with his last comment. "Well you take care and be safe out here". "I will, Sir", I replied as I packed the last of my gear onto the R6.

Treading in Confusion

I resolved to do tarot readings by donation and see if I could drum up enough cash to ensure dinner was going to happen. I also could hang out in the park again and try my best to make more connections with the less scary-looking people in the park. It was obvious that they were used to living rough and I was the prissy bitch who came in on a brand new motorcycle. Even here, appearances have their effect on people, yet every day my own grime became more and more apparent. In an odd way, I was transforming into the thing I needed to be. I had worn the same pair of pants for the last five days straight and had operated without a shower for three days. I used a bottle of cold water to wet a t-shirt I decided to sacrifice for bathing and soaped it up with some lavender hippie soap. Only the essential parts of my body got attention: my junk, so I wouldn't smell like balls and ass, and my feet so my tent wouldn't stink when I took off my socks at night. Though it seemed so ghetto, I again felt good, really good, like I was being something I couldn't have been before. I had been changing to adapt to my conditions. This is what practitioners of magic say is the greatest magical act, to be able to transform at will. Having never really done anything like this before, it was all very real, very stern and yet I still held onto some kind of blind hope, a feeling that if I was patient and grateful, the universe would be willing to throw me a mulligan. Now that the coffee and charging spot had been established I planned to use the very last of my credit to buy a single baguette of bread if no other meals presented themselves to me.

I couldn't help but think about the Cathar perfecti who would travel around spreading their gnostic message. They were not allowed to have money, because it was a vice to their faith that would cause them to lust after the world of fleshly satisfaction. They were however obligated to help anyone who asked them for help. They only ate rice, or other unseasoned, plant-based foods, just enough for sustenance and not a bite more. I considered what they did and a wave of gratefulness washed over me. As I contemplated the perfecti, my phone rang. It was Baby Jesus. He said he was in town and wanted to hang out with me. I told him I was out of cash and he offered to buy me lunch for the pleasure of my company. At that very moment I couldn't help but wonder what factor my gratefulness played in this tiny gift from the universe.

As I sat and waited for Baby Jesus to show up, I tried to focus on all of the blessings I had in my life: my son, Gideon, who was so smart and talented at virtually everything he did; Gwyneth, my sweet daughter, joyful and rambunctious, whose love for everything and everyone shined like a beacon through any dark time I've ever had. I thought about my friends, Albert and Macy, who gave me shelter when there was none, and their offerings of red wine and good conversation. I thought about my LA friends, Hank, Tahoe, and Robert, who

Treading in Confusion

all offered help to me in any situation. I thought about my step-mom and my dad, who always kept an eye on me to make sure I was okay. I thought about my friend and colleague, Dr. August, who had helped me to get accepted into the University of Philosophical Research and provided me with much balanced wisdom and support.

I wasn't mad at my friends whose offers of connections fell through; rather I took it as a sign, a bit of a stretch that needed to happen. I looked at the tattoo on my right arm of a koi fish with two gold coins in its mouth. For the first time in a long time I remembered what those gold coins meant; I would always have just enough to do what needs to be done. I felt the same way as I ate that baguette, "give us this day our daily bread". I knew that I could project my own magic enough to keep a bright light on for anyone looking for somebody good. I knew that something would come despite a situation that others might see as totally disastrous. While sitting at Luke's Joint waiting for Baby Jesus I drew my three-card tarot spread for the day. Card one: King of Chalices—moral authority; help and lessons; protection and guidance. Card two: King of Wands, inverted—austerity and ambiguousness. Card three: Seven of Wands, inverted—anxiety and confusion. It seemed like the universe was offering me a warning not to give in to the dangers of the present. The spread told me there would be protection even through the austerity and the temptation to be confused and anxious.

Baby Jesus arrived with a smile and a handshake and began straightaway to talk about his new web database for those seeking enlightenment and education. We plotted and planned on his grand idea, which I truly enjoyed. He offered to run me to the grocery store so I could have food for the next couple of days. I couldn't refuse. Jesus explained to me how he had on many an occasion been stuck without help and was granted a boon by the gods by way of the kindness of strangers. He thought it a noble deed to pay it forward just because he could. I told him that he was my own personal Jesus. He laughed with a squinty face, which looked quite charming on him. It felt like everyday was filled with just enough miracle to keep things going and Baby Jesus played a big part in that.

Jesus offered to loan me some cash if I found myself in a desperate situation, to which I offered my thanks. He also said he might have work for both of us soon and that he would let me know. It just blew me away that I had started this day planning to eat nothing but cold oatmeal in the morning, a dozen cups of coffee and one baguette, and now I had four bananas, two apples, two pears, a jar of peanut butter, bread, more oatmeal, and a bunch of cacao nuggets. Was it my charm that did the trick? Was it my magic? Was it simply the odd unwarranted kindness of Baby Jesus? Whatever it was, it was a welcome sign and hopefully a bellwether for the rest of this adventure.

Treading in Confusion

I took the food back to my encampment and began to set up my tent. This time there were other campers, though they opted to set up down on the beach. I decided to stay put since my motorcycle was my only salvation at this point, as far as my ability to get in or out of situations was concerned. As I wrapped up, a man with a big ol' bulldog came up to me to say hi. He offered me a cold beer and stood by my bike. "I've got a 650 touring bike in my trailer. We should go for a ride soon". "Well", I said, "that all depends on how my migrant-working venture pans out; so far I've been here four days and haven't found any work". "Oh man, there is money to be made everywhere out here, you just gotta know the right people. Truth be told, I just moved here to oversee an operation". "Well", I said, "I'd be happy to join your crew if you have any need of extra workers". I offered my card to him and handed him a copy of my first book, *Riding The Fine Line*. He thumbed through it as he told me how he made eight grand the week before. "It's crazy, I just called up a couple of friends who buy by the pound and before you know it, I have eight grand".

I tried not to press too hard for work, but after four days of nothing I was ready to do what I came here to do. As we shook hands I told him to google me to make sure I was who I said I was. He drove off promising to see what he could do to get me in. I'd grown weary of promises as far as this was concerned and resolved to let it happen if it happened, or not. Either way it seemed there was a spot waiting for me somewhere in the right place and the right time. Some lovely surfer girls walked by in their wetsuits in the moonlight, having had an early evening surf session. I couldn't help but feel a little tinge of desire. It had been a while since I'd had the warmth of a woman and there was no real promise anywhere in sight. But as quickly as the thought came it went, and I finished wrapping up the setup of my tent.

Now that some time had passed, I had become accustomed to my small two-person tent and organized everything perfectly. This night I had put the tarp inside of the tent doubled up underneath my sleeping bag in order to soften the bruising that I had on either hip from lying on the ground. My bag of groceries sat beside me like a giant gold victory cup, or at least that's how it felt after a series of humbling realities had chilled my verve for this venture. Now things were on the up and up, I had met some people who might actually be able to help me, I had gotten food and gas. For the moment I had more than I needed and that was all that mattered to me.

It's funny, only weeks before I had spent night after night with insomniac terrors and worries about what I was going to do to please somebody else and their vision of what happiness looked like. Now I was sleeping like a baby against the earth herself. The bills, the parking tickets, the woes and worries of everyone running around like

Treading in Confusion

busy bees had nothing on me as I lay just a millimeter from the cool, fertile soil of the Northern California woods. What was I doing? I was doing what I was supposed to do, even though it didn't look like what people expected it to look like. My vision was my own for the first time and I say the first time because only now have I known myself well enough to make this kind of calculated risk, to venture out into the cold dark night and not only survive, but thrive. Our worried mothers warn us to take every precaution, but sometimes we just have to let those mothers worry.

There is a life to be lived out here on the highway and in the middle of nowhere. There is a flower that blooms only for those brave enough to seek it out in the misty hills. I hadn't placed my trimming scissors to a single bud of weed yet and already I felt like a new man, victorious and capable of anything. Why was this? I hadn't really done much other than trust a blind whim and leverage all my bargaining chips in hopes of a big win, but there I was in the heart of the forest, singing a quiet song of contentment, just my tent, my bike, and me.

Chapter 4

YET ANOTHER DAY ARRIVED WITHOUT A guaranteed work plan. I went back to Luke's because I had now built a good reputation with the staff and they knew the drill. They knew exactly why I was there and what I was up to; but I don't roll like some nefarious character, I roll like Gabe, a ball of sunshine.

In walked Baby Jesus with a red bandana on his head, looking more the pirate than ever before. He loved that I wasn't just on some drug kick for the sake of drugs. In fact, I wasn't really on drugs at all. I was too busy trying to find work to think about being lit. We spent most of the early afternoon jawboning about his website plan and decided that we both needed to do laundry. The money that Albert and Macy had wired me had come through sooner than I had expected and it afforded me the luxury of doing laundry. After five days roughing it, my pants could have walked off on their own, so it was a blessing to be able to wrangle them into a washing machine and make them clean again.

I gave Baby Jesus a copy of my first book as a gift and a token of my gratitude, since while we were washing our clothes he bought a pizza pie for us to share. It's rare to find the kind of generosity that Baby Jesus so effortlessly offered to me. It was what I would have classically called "grace" in my Christian days. Here it was, religion-free and gracious as fuck. Wonderful.

Before heading back to my campsite, I thought I'd venture a bit further north just to enjoy my perfect R6. She sang through the turns of the 101 until I decided to check out a rest stop. I pulled up and parked, locked the bike, and walked into the woods. As I followed the path, the tall, majestic trees breathed out a little more oxygen just for me. It was silent with placid life, stoic and full of energy, green and crisp. I stepped off the path and felt the ground beneath me soften as if to invite me in. I walked in about twenty yards and just stood there with my eyes closed, allowing myself to be in the moment. This was a gift richer than anything money could buy; it was a glimpse of paradise.

After I had silenced myself, I headed back to the path and made my way to the men's room, the nicest one I'd ever seen at a rest stop. I used the opportunity to change into my freshly washed pants and give myself another spot wash. I got back on the R6 and gave a hard pull on the throttle. She sprang happily to my request, coming to highway speed in milliseconds. I rode up to a national park

Treading in Confusion

and looked for a new place to camp, but like everywhere else it was fifteen to twenty dollars just to post up. This was maddening to me and led me once again to ask: how is this the land of the free when there is no place to rest your head for free?

I made my way back to Trinidad where I could still abuse the loophole spot that didn't happen to have a "No Camping" sign. After setting up my tent, I decided that tonight was the night I would pick up a bottle of wine. I grabbed the cheapest non-shitty wine I could find: "Our Daily Red". I grabbed a small pack of baby wipes and made my way back to the camp. Even with the hope and promise of work to come, it still felt like I had failed in some fashion. Perhaps it wasn't that at all, but the messages that had come through hearsay about what my ex was saying about me. I couldn't let that get to me, because truth be told, whatever suffering I might have endured presently, it was better than the unhappiness that had become my daily life with her. I unscrewed the top of the wine bottle and put on the new Queens of the Stone Age album on my smartphone. The song rang out with a powerful melancholy that coupled well with the wine. The nearly full moon crept out past the tree line and greeted me with her pale luminescence. I sang to the moon, bottle in hand, trying to stave off a sorrow of indiscernible cause, perhaps a mélange of all I had been through and was still going through. Most of all it was the pale cold chill of being alone.

Morning came and I greeted the sun with a moment of silence in its gilded rays, allowing the warmth to permeate my whole body. The blue veil of the night fled like an exorcised demon and was replaced with an ecstatic energy that filled me up. I was bathed in the glory of Ra. I packed up my gear after deciding to lighten my load. One pair of swimming trunks that had seen too many years and a t-shirt I had used to wash my ass for two days were sent to the trash. I moved my rain gear into my roll-up tent setup to further lighten my backpack. No matter where I went, I had to have my big backpack on me, because it contained everything I owned: laptop, passport, old phone, clothes, charging adapters and cords, weed, asthma meds, and personal hygiene products. I felt good as I made my way back into town.

Luke's Joint had issues with their card reader and were cash only on this day. I opted for a café across the square as an alternative. After ordering a coffee and a breakfast sandwich, I pulled out my Golden Klimt tarot deck. I'd been getting days and days of shitty readings with themes like, entrapment, austerity, broken promises, loss of friends, betrayal, and so on. Today I hoped for something better, and as I shuffled the cards, I begged for something good. The spread was as follows: Nine of Pentacles – financial windfall, new beginnings and new love. Ten of Chalices—sharing, community and friendship. The Wheel—financial gain, prudent decision-making, and success. Upon read-

Treading in Confusion

ing the spread I threw both fists in the air and yelled, "yes!" not really caring who heard or saw me. Moments after, Ben texted me, "Hey dude, I'm in the hills cutting down some new stuff. I'm putting in a good word to get you up here to work". With the close proximity of timing I took it as a sign, but I couldn't make any assumptions until I was actually working.

I ended up talking to the guy sitting next to me who was obviously also up here to do some work in the hills. We exchanged stories about how fickle connections can be and how good it was to travel on your own. We talked about what would be the ideal thing to do, maybe to buy some land and build some cheap housing with friends and make it into something everyone could be excited about. Why was it so goddamned hard to just live? Why did we have to take part in the meat grinder? What's the better thing to do, to talk about change and how we should do this or that, or to actually do it? It left a desire in my heart and possibly sparked a stronger will to buy property if I had enough money to do so. With my phone and computer nearly dead, I decided to head over to the bank and pull out my last full twenty so I could hang out at Luke's and charge my stuff. I said goodbye to my chatting companion and made my way over to Luke's.

A coffee was two dollars and twenty-five cents, so it wasn't too big of an investment to charge everything up and it made a nice environment for writing. Most importantly, I could do all of this while having a direct view of my R6 so I could ensure she wasn't getting fucked with by drunken vagrants. I trusted that my cards wouldn't lie to me since they accurately predicted my troubles. Why wouldn't they assist me with the good news as well? At two-thirty Baby Jesus walked in. We hadn't planned on meeting, but I was fairly predictable in my patterns. He expressed his eagerness to get back up in the hills to work as well. I tried my best to mitigate my five days of angst about not having work and just keep to the pleasant conversation. I realized that Baby Jesus was a living mile-marker of sorts. I'd only known him for a couple of days, but even after that, I couldn't imagine life without knowing him. He was my tie to this world of which I was a stranger, but more than that, he had become somebody I could trust to be true in a time and place where everyone else had lacked any follow through.

Though he was nearly a decade younger than me, he had a breadth of knowledge that I did not, much of it in heavy eastern philosophy. He taught yoga and practiced it for two hours per day. He was the perfect pirate, burner, yogic young master who wanted to show the world something beautiful. Older generations always complain about the younger ones, but this is an illusion of the jaded. True, many people are stone stupid, but many others are using every advantage they have to learn and master what they love. They are becoming

Treading in Confusion

highly specialized in a way that is totally foreign to older generations. Baby Jesus had a mission of his own and I did what I could to add to his vision, though I must admit I'd been teetering between total freedom and total collapse, emotionally. Here, this dude who had literally fed me and made sure I was okay was now keeping me company in my time of utmost loneliness. Whether he knew it or not, his presence in my life was one of the kindest gifts the universe had sent me in recent memory.

No news came in regard to work and we parted ways. I headed back to Trinidad and set up my tent, bumping "Guns of Brixton" as I got everything situated. Dinner consisted of tipping a jar of peanut butter deftly so that it spread across my bread evenly, then pulling and twisting it so that it would taper just perfectly to prevent a spill. I still didn't have proper utensils or cleaning supplies, so I had to try to perform acts of unimaginable skill in order to avoid a mess. I hadn't really ventured out to where the ocean was because I was always preoccupied with protecting my earthly possessions, but I figured it might do me some good to walk down the trail that everyone else seemed to enjoy. After about eighty yards, the path turned left and ran parallel to a cliff that overlooked the most breathtaking cove I had seen since I had visited the road to Hana in Maui. The sky was hot pink with darker hues of violet and blue. The flat plane of the ocean was broken up by monolithic outcroppings of stone that reached forty feet into the air; their tops were crowned by fierce evergreens that stretched even further up. When I saw this I wished I had someone there with me to share the moment, so I called my kids and checked in to see how they were doing. My son was enjoying school spirit week while my daughter was all excited about learning division. Personally I couldn't think of anything more horrifying than having to do math work all over again. Having checked in and letting them know I was enjoying 'camping' I hung up the phone. For a while I just sat on the concrete picnic table beside my tent and listened to some music.

As the twilight turned to dark, the full moon began to blast its hypnotic light down upon everything, making the ominous forest look more lush than gothic. My visit to the outhouse some eighty yards from the tent was less exciting. With a flashlight in my mouth I ventured over and stepped in and looked up to see a big spider with some kind of skull pattern on its back. I assumed this was a sign that it was not the kind I should make my pet. Then I made the unfortunate mistake of looking all around to find the whole outhouse was some kind of spider convention. It made it difficult to relax enough to relieve myself. I got out of there as quickly as I could, preferring to risk death by werewolf over death by toilet spider. Now night after night, the lonely dark swept over me like a cold blanket, silently wearing at my will and good spirits. I knew though that good news may already

Treading in Confusion

be in the works, and I clung to that very thought through the dark as I nestled into my tiny tent once again.

The cold seemed inescapable and I tried to fight it with all the resources that I had. I used a Mylar emergency blanket as a base for the tent and draped the tarp over the top of the tent, hoping that this combination would trap my body heat better. It wasn't the midnight hour, but about three or four AM that would test whether or not this scheme would work.

Now it was my custom to take a couple hits of Tahoe, not just because it helped me fall asleep, but because I longed for some light intervention and comfort that came from the gentle intoxication this particular strain brought. I was of sound mind, but my mind had worries and a little Tahoe really helped at the time. I turned on the music quietly for a couple of songs and paid attention to every word, focusing like a meditation on it so that I could just let go of my worry. Off it went until I groggily turned the sound off and sleep took me away.

Chapter 5

BEFORE THIS ADVENTURE HAD BEGUN I WAS without daily work for months on end, and it had already taken its toll on my self-esteem. Now I was on a veritable one-way ticket to permanent camping by myself, and it was just too much. I felt like I was ready to break. The loss of a six-year relationship, regardless of whether it was good or bad, plus the lack of gainful employment, brought on a deep, dark sadness that I had trouble shaking. My eyes wanted to cry, but they couldn't. Perhaps if I could afford enough wine to get good and shit-faced I could generate a cry, but it wasn't gonna happen. Instead, the pain just sat there collecting around the edges of my eyes, glazing over me like algæ on a submerged oceanic stone, causing anything that strode upon it to slip into the cold.

A simple call, a single text, a friendly word from a pretty girl, anything could lift me up, but it just wasn't there. The words didn't happen, the message didn't come, and I was invisible to this town. I sent the message I didn't want to send—

to ask for some money. I was sure that there was still a fortune to be made, but I needed more time and time meant money. My closest friend in New York, Zeb, called and told me to hang in there. He told me about how lonely he had felt while he was on his motorcycle ride across the west and midwest. "Nobody can really understand what it means to be alone like that until they actually go. Once they go, they know".

I used the last of my cash to buy a baguette and a block of mozzarella. As a bonus I was also able to afford two apples. I cut the baguette in half and again lengthwise so I could cram it full of cheese. As I chowed down on my sandwich, I looked across the park and saw the fella I had chatted with the day before. I walked over to him as he sat shirtless in the sun with his braided beard and ponytail. It's either Ryan or Bryan, I said as I walked up to him with a smile. He offered a handshake, "It's Ryan, good to see you again!" I sat down beside him and noted that just moments before, a homeless woman had been arrested by the cops. "Yeah, I've been taking photos of the police brutality here and cataloguing it. I'm an activist making sure people get treated fairly. This town doesn't even have a public bathroom". I chimed in how I had noticed there wasn't much in the way of public services and how easy one could find themselves needing to shit in an alleyway. "That's just it, there's no sense of humanity in this. What's better, to make people have to do something like that rather than have

Treading in Confusion

a safe and clean place to take care of their basic needs?" Because I was on the fringe of being homeless myself, I began to understand what I hadn't really understood before. I didn't have an actual address, I didn't have a job, I didn't have any money, and I was quasi-illegally sleeping in a tent in the woods and washing my ass in a honey bucket. I finally grasped on a new level what it was like for this experience to be one's only reality.

Ryan was right; we did treat homeless people like shit because there just wasn't enough demand for proper decency. Not every homeless person is a drug addict or alcoholic; many people are legitimately out of luck. I looked around at the people in the park: runaway kids who obviously needed medical attention for mental disorders; a haggard woman with bandages on her face from having it bashed in by somebody the night before; another man with his wrist broken from a similar incident. People were in need. A more sinister part of me hoped this whole society would just finally relieve us all and turn to shit so that the playing field was equal, so that all those dickheads in their brand new ninety-thousand dollar cars and McMansions would have to wash their balls in an outhouse forever. Of course this thought passed, but the sense of how easy it could be to lose one's humanity became a reality to me. If the world hates you and treats you like you don't matter, like they hope you stop existing, then why shouldn't you hate those motherfuckers back?

Despite the heavy conversation and surroundings, Ryan had a genuinely positive outlook. He was one of those people whose energy was so bright and wonderful that he might as well have glowed in the dark. We sat and chatted a bit more until the sky turned grey and it got cold. Ryan opted to head to the grocery store and get some food, and I decided to head back to my encampment. Riding up, the chill in the air became a bit more wicked, and I was shaking by the time I got to Trinidad. I threw on an extra t-shirt and added my sweater. I cut up the other half of the baguette I had from lunch and added the remaining cheese as well as half of a sliced-up apple. It was quite lovely and nearly good enough to serve at a French restaurant. I devoured it with joy and after the last bite got the tent all set up.

Sitting once again in the tent wasn't fun or exciting anymore. It looked more like a spacious coffin than a rustic escape from the norm. I fucking hated it and hated that I was stuck here. I let my bad attitude out in the silence since I had to return the next day with my shit-eating grin trying to find work, but for now in the dark, I scowled like a savage. This cocktail of depression over no work, sadness over a failed relationship, and the plain and simple loneliness of being alone just made me feel horrible. If I could have had the chance to give up then and there, I might have taken it, but fate had other plans.

¶

*In the clear light
of the setting sun,
if not beating a pot
and singing,
then you will be making
the lament of great old age.
Pitfall.*

I CHING, HEXAGRAM 30, LINE 3

Chapter 6

I MADE MY WAY INTO TOWN IN A MANNER that had become habitual, though this time I had no cash. The money Zeb wired had not come through yet, so I went without my usual gallon of coffee. Instead I posted up on the southwestern corner of the town square and used my last slice of bread to get the last of the peanut butter out of the jar. I sat there thinking grumbly thoughts, worrying about a situation that seemed out of my control. By the time I had finished eating my peanut butter and bread, I noticed a girl that I had seen a week before sitting on a blanket on the other side of the square.

I made my way over and called out, "little Texas! You're from Texas, right?" "No", she replied, "I'm from Mississippi. How are you doing today? I have stones for sale!" I wondered to myself what she meant by stones; was it some kind of exotic drug I had never heard of? Was it a term for huge nuggets of mutant weed? She pulled out a box and revealed a dozen or more precious stones, pieces of petrified wood, trilobites, and other lovely stones. The mystery had been revealed; she meant actual stones.

Her travel companion, another southern girl, sat down and put out a red quinoa salad with barbeque sauce. They offered for me to dig in and since I hadn't had anything other than peanut butter on dry bread, I dug in. As we munched on the unique snack, we ended up talking about the machine elves of Terence McKenna fame.

For those who are not aware, McKenna, the most important voice on psychedelics in the last 25 years, described the experience, especially the kind found in the tryptamine-based psychedelics such as mushrooms and DMT, as one that is alien in nature. Often in these experiences, entities are encountered that he described as "self transforming machine elves".

I told them about my first DMT experience in which I met them: I had tried a couple of runs with DMT, but felt like I was in the waiting room for some other, grander experience. I finally got the proper apparatus for consuming it properly and took a big breath in. As I held my breath I felt myself falling up and out of myself, thrust into a foreign visual landscape in which everything was moving and spinning and turning in on itself like a waterfall that fell in a repeating figure eight. There were other beings there that seemed more familiar to me than anyone I had met in the regular world. They were like my long lost friends; they didn't look like people, but rather roiling balls of technicolor energy that rolled like an active Celtic knot that wouldn't hold still. They bounded up to me, spilling over one another, showing me wonder upon wonder with such urgency that it was difficult to keep up.

It was comparable to being a Fortune 500 executive who has been out of the office for six months. Your staff has been diligently holding down the fort for you, but the paperwork has really stacked up and many decisions must be made. Imagine walking into that office for only ten minutes and trying to cram six months of catch-up work in that amount of time. The machine elves kept yelling that we had so much work to do. Then, as I floated back down, these eternal friends of sorts waved goodbye, telling me to come back so we could get to work. As I looked up from my description of my DMT trip, both girls looked at me with eyes like saucers. "That gave me chills!" one girl cried; the other agreed empathetically. I noticed in them a kind of hopeful generosity of listening. They didn't know me at all, and yet they were gracious enough to open themselves up to the weirdness of my story and share in the kind of star-struck wonder that we were all seeking to experience.

At that point my phone rang, it was Baby Jesus. He was standing less than twenty feet from me looking the opposite direction, obviously looking for me. "Where are you? Oh! Right here!" He caught me waving at him as he hung up his phone and came over. "Man, guys, I walked in the redwoods and I feel so much better about things. I'd been getting caught up in worry about getting more work. I realized all this will come and go. It was really freeing to just sit among the trees and listen to them".

I stood up and excused myself from the blanket we were sitting on and Baby Jesus took me over to the pizza place. He knew I was out of cash again and also in need of food. We sat and talked about how Helena Blavatsky was the unsung hero of the movement of consciousness and eastern thought being introduced to the west. She had founded the Theosophical Society in 1875 and wrote the seminal book, *Isis Unveiled*. Like many people who start organizations with good intentions, Helena's vision had become tarnished by the bad choices of lesser leaders once she had passed on. Many people blamed Blavatsky for eugenics, the Nazi master race, and other gems of the twentieth century, but truth be told, the only master race she spoke of was one in which all of humanity would unite as a great blending of all races.

Anyone who bothered to read her material would discover that she spoke about compassion and education as the highest virtues, as well as a rejection of fleshly desire in favor of a spiritually pure life. Baby Jesus and I laughed about how we make monsters out of good people and good people out of monsters.

Beating a Pot & Singing

The time passed faster than either of us had noticed and Baby Jesus offered to help me out with groceries for a second time. He thanked me for sharing my thoughts, which seemed to have a synchronistic effect upon him. Little comments I made here and there lit him up like a Christmas tree, and he glowed with the face of one who had reached an epiphany. We walked down the street and across the town square to the food co-op where I wrangled a big bag of mixed nuts, a new jar of peanut butter, and some bread. I threw in four pears to the basket and called it good. Baby Jesus was again my own personal Jesus. "You know, Gabe, maybe if you meditated more, you wouldn't be so stressed out about finding work. I mean look at you! You're all beautiful! You gotta get dirty man. You look like a federal agent!" I pulled off my five-dollar frames, which apparently looked like Versace, and tussled my hair and added a stupid look on my face. "That's more like it! I'd hire you in a second!" I retorted to his jab about meditation. You know, Baby Jesus, I meditated for twenty minutes this morning among the trees. I've got a lot of really big changes going on in my life and I'm trying to hold it together. You're right though, I don't have any excuse about not taking the time to get deeper in my own personal practice. I need to be able to dig deeper. I took Jesus's jab to heart because I knew there was some weight to it. Once again, I was the spiritual or deep guy talking about stuff on an intellectual level, but not fully taking it in on the physical and practical scale. I still had much to learn, but the lessons I was deep in still had plenty of sting.

We decided to meet up the next day during the farmers market in the square. We'd make a cardboard sign that advertised we were looking for work and just chill out. I had assumed that Zeb's money would come through by then and I would be able to relax for at least a day. If no work came my way, I could always take a chance and ride out to Weaverville, deeper in the hills of Humboldt. I didn't really have a handle on any of this anymore. I was disillusioned by my friends and being graciously watched over by Baby Jesus, so I couldn't tell if my mission was blessed or cursed. I opted for the blessing, trying to keep my attitude on the up and up. Nobody was going to hire a scowling jerk anyway.

I rode back north to Trinidad in the thick fog, a real chill setting in as it did the day before. When I got in I set up the tent quickly and in a new spot since somebody had left a huge dog turd where I had camped the night before. A cute jogger girl made her way past me on her way into the woods. I walked over to the outhouse and spent some time there. As I came out, she was there again on her way back out of the park. How's the run? I asked. "Oh, great. I see you're camping here alone. Will you be here for a couple of days?" I've been here for a week. "Well, me and my girlfriends live just around the corner and come out to drink cham-

Beating a Pot & Singing

pagne sometimes. Maybe we will come see you". Come by anytime, I said. There were immediately several visions that I had come to me after her comment. I imagined three or four college age girls whacking each other with pillows and laughing. What should we do now? I know! Let's head over to that hot dude camping and get drunk with him! Maybe we can bring him back here to our warm house full of food and have a naked party! These thoughts obviously were not those of a sane man, but a man hanging big imagination on little comments. It had been a while since I'd been with a woman and just a simple remark could spark an avalanche of thought.

Chapter 7

I WOKE UP AT SIX AM WITH A MESSAGE FROM my ex. She had received a letter from me and expressed gratitude for some clarification. She now understood, and told me that we could work on ending the relationship amiably. I wrote back and told her that I needed some space and silence in order to regain some of the dignity that I had lost over time. I couldn't sleep after that. I had to use the bathroom but didn't want to get up. I wanted to cry after reading her words. Nobody wants to hurt others, or at least I didn't want to, but what can you do when you are insanely unhappy? At some point you have to let go if you don't want to end up twenty years down the road with bitterness so deep that it would poison your whole life.

I called my dad and talked to him a bit about my status. He and my stepmother were concerned about my condition and wanted to make sure I was okay. I reassured them I was on the up and up despite the lack of work so far. My assurances put their worry to rest for the time being anyway.

I rode into town for the farmer's market and set-up a cardboard sign that said, "free tarot readings" on one side and "looking for work" on the other. The looking for work sign had a little pot leaf symbol just to make it more obvious. Several people came up and got readings. Most everyone expressed gratitude about the readings. It seemed the fucking tarot cards worked for everyone but me! After about ten readings I had earned enough money from donations to get my first hot meal in four days. I instinctually went to Luke's and got a pulled pork soup bowl. I devoured it in less than two minutes. I thought about all the people who are looking for a sense of direction and how a little thing like a tarot reading really seemed to make a difference in their spirits.

It was getting old going up to Trinidad, but I wasn't feeling well and I needed to get some rest. I set up my tent as soon as I got there, lay down, and closed my eyes. I felt feverish but wasn't sure if I was actually sick. My feeling ill may have had something to do with me eating three peanut butter sandwiches as my dinner. The peanut butter sat like a brick in my stomach, making me queasy. With a couple of hours of just laying there, I started to feel better. I woke in the morning to a voice, "You in the tent, wake up". I knew before I looked that it was a park ranger. "You need to pack up your gear and leave. You can't just camp anywhere you want". I didn't see any no camping signs, sir, my apologies, I replied. He noted some

Beating a Pot & Singing

obscure sign that was literally a mile down the road from where my campsite was. It wasn't even on the same road. "I'm not going to give you a citation, but it's a misdemeanor to illegally camp. There's nowhere that you can camp for free except at the rest stops along the 101, otherwise it has to be a designated camping area". I respectfully nodded and told the officer that I didn't camp very often and was unaware of this fact. He told me to be gone by sunset, but since my tent fell over as I got out nervously, I figured getting out sooner than later was a good idea. I packed up my stuff and got on the bike. I wondered if he felt bad that there wasn't any real place for people to camp. I wondered if he thought it was okay that you had to pay to live. I was worried about my fuel and food situation, because I was up to ninety-nine miles on a 120 mile capacity tank before the fuel light goes on. I opted to go into town to maybe hustle up some tarot work for cash, or maybe try to run my maxed credit card.

As I got into town, the fuel light came on and I rolled into a gas station. I put my credit card in and ran it. Approved! I filled the R6 up as much as it could go and made my way over to Luke's, hoping my maxed card would still work for some food. After the peanut butter incident I had decided to lay off the jar. I walked into Luke's and asked them to run my card for their most expensive sandwich plate and a coffee. They did and it was again accepted. I had just now gotten food and gas. I pulled out my tarot cards and ran my spread: Four of Swords, Two of Chalices, and the Ace of Pentacles. In other words, money, cash, hoes. I really hoped that today was indeed that the universe would at least keep one of these promises.

All these shenanigans with the cops and free places to stay really hit home to me. I did after all have a warm bed waiting for me in three locations if I so chose to finagle my way there, but many people don't. Many people are one missed payment away from foreclosure, one mistake at work from a career job that won't come back. We're all one more financial collapse from America the beautiful to Cormac McCarthy's *The Road*. So when the shit hits the fan and nobody can afford a pot to piss in, what's going to happen then? When people who are willing to work can't find work, will they end up as a reject like the people they despise, those vermin on the side of the road holding cardboard signs? Being a person who was now the proud owner of a cardboard sign myself, I understood the cold hard lie that the American dream was. You're only invited if you want to play the game, or if you're savvy enough to keep a corporate job, but stupid enough to think it couldn't go away in a heartbeat. One day, we're Marie Antoinette, the next we're headed for the guillotine, but we're still oblivious and high on the hog, eating the sweet cakes of the world suffering under our feet and laughing as we fix our powdered wigs in the mirror. America has become the bane of this planet, and we don't even

Beating a Pot & Singing

know it. This is my beautiful country where we are free in songs, but not in reality, noble in our ideals, but not in our actions. We love Jesus, but we despise the poor.

As I ruminated over my leveraged meal, I watched a police officer clear the park of the usual suspects. Anyone who resisted would be arrested. In this little town of Arcata, they would only tolerate you so long before they charge the poor fines for being poor. It made me sick to see and I wasn't too far away by distance, or by situation. None of us really are. This distance we have between us and the rest of humanity is an illusion that will not always hypnotize us. The question lies in when we will break free of the illusion, when we ourselves are balls deep in calamity, or right now as we decide between living in love, or fear.

Ben had sent me a message saying that I should head south about seventy-five miles and that it would be a better spot. He told me that he had work in the next week or so, but I could also probably find work there quite easily just hanging out on the street. Having spent eight days in Arcata, I was ready to try something new. I had been hanging on a shoestring for days and days, and had a full tank of gas. How much worse could it be to be down and out in another city? I got on the bike and she immediately thanked me for getting back up to speed for duration. The R6 sang happily to me through the twists and turns of the emerald forests of the 101. I blasted, "Go With The Flow" in my headphones as I cruised along and sang aloud to every word. Before I knew it I was in the town I was told to go to and pulled up to a gas station and filled up, having once again leveraged my maxed credit card. I pulled up to another gas station to get a look of the town and saw Ben walking down the street. Ben! I yelled out. He turned and saw me and smiled. He crossed the street and we both commented on how weird it was that as soon as I got in town he was nearly the first person that I had seen. We walked over to the grocery store where he was picking up some things for the people he worked for.

Though he had already made it clear that he didn't presently have work for me, I considered it a fortuitous occasion that he would be there right as I pulled up. It seemed that my journey had been vouchsafed and that I was on the right track despite the quasi-nefarious nature of this venture. He explained to me the problem with the weed business in California: It's legal to grow weed as long as the quantity matches the number of people living on the farm with green cards, but it is illegal for one person to transport pounds of weed to the dispensaries. It's legal for the dispensaries to sell the weed to those who have a green card, but there is a grey area between the grower and the dispensary. This is where the money is made. Those brave enough to face a jail sentence for transit reap big bucks getting the weed illegally from one legal spot to the other. It's totally stupid. After

Beating a Pot & Singing

I walked with him as he gathered his groceries, he handed me a twenty dollar bill. This was the second person and the third time that someone had just handed me a gift of money or food. I expressed my gratitude and we parted ways. I thought at first of going to a restaurant, but then I opted to buy bread, cheese, and meat for a sandwich. I grabbed a bottle of wine as well, paid for it, then headed to a small park that Ben had told me about.

When I got to the park, I sat down and pulled out the sourdough loaf and cut it down the side with my designated food knife. Then I cut the small Roma tomato I had bought and placed the slices along the loaf. I placed my tarot readings sign up in case somebody wanted a reading. Some people shuffled in and out while I ate my sandwich, but then some dude came in describing the situation in this town. "Yeah, everyone knows why all these travelers are here, so they make sure they charge a shitload for camping and places to stay. I've got six people and two dogs staying in a room with me tonight". I asked him if he wanted a reading, "No, that's okay, but let me ask you this, what color was the garage of your childhood home?" I turned my head to the right and was about to say white, but before I could, he said, "aha! You're an artistic analytical type! See, you turned your head in the direction of the side of your brain that you use the most. I got you man, I knew you were like me!" I smiled amusedly over his parlor trick, which was admittedly better than any that I had.

I decided to scope out places to sleep since I had no idea what I was doing. I rode just north of town and into the Humboldt State Park. I pulled in to see if there was a place I could stealth camp at, but I found something better. As I took my helmet off and walked into the park, I found myself beset on all sides by trees so tall, it was difficult to estimate their height. Their average width was better than two of me at full arms length. A sense of awe swept over me, something akin to the fear of god. I was washed with terror and trembling because I knew I stood on holy ground. In the distance I heard the angelic, melodious sound of a fiddle echoing through the woods. This wasn't a dream, or a movie. I followed the broad trail and scaled massive logs to see off into the distance the shape of a man passionately playing his instrument. I thought at first to go sit in front of him and listen, but I didn't want to ruin the moment. Instead I just looked up at the trees to this forlorn and brooding soundtrack, simply blown away and overwhelmed by what my eyes couldn't even fully grasp. Life was beautiful.

Still needing to find a place to sleep I drove a little further down the road and discovered a spot where stumps were put up, but a bike could fit. I stopped and explored the space. It had clearly been camped in before, but it was in a dark and remote spot where nightfall would make it even more foreboding. I thought about setting up then and there, but became paranoid after the morn-

Beating a Pot & Singing

ing's run in with the law. The sun was setting, but I didn't have the guts to try setting up, so I went back into town and looked around. Everything seemed closed up and dismal. After another round, I decided to invest myself in the secret spot past the redwoods.

When I got there I switched off the bike and let it coast in neutral into the forest. I had done it without being noticed. As I began to set up my tent in the blackness of the forest I heard two men talking like they were walking either in the woods or along the road. I showed a light so that my presence would be known. But as soon as I did this, the conversation fell silent. I stood with the light off again, listening for a single sound of a footstep, anything to let me know they were continuing on, but I heard nothing. I stood there for a good three minutes just listening in the dark, my gear strewn all over the ground. A car drove past on the road just out of sight from where I was setting up and after it passed I heard a large crack of a branch less than fifteen yards from me. I shone my light in the direction and announced myself. "I'm just a camper, please just announce yourself so I know you are there". Nothing. Not a sound.

Chapter 8

AT THIS POINT MY MIND WAS RACING and I imagined two husky guys with guns or knives ready to jump me as soon as I had relaxed. With haste I gathered up my stuff and threw it all together, all the while checking in a 360 degree pattern to ensure nobody snuck up on me. My fixed blade was at my hip and I was ready to use it if I had to. Once everything was on board the R6, I turned it on and skidded my way out of that black hole in the forest.

I still needed a place to stay and was no closer to a solution. I parked outside of a gas station along the only main road in town. There were gritty gutter punks and hippies everywhere, none of which seemed to have a place to stay. My bike had been my salvation but also a burden because I couldn't just sleep in my car; I had to guard the bike so nobody would steal it. If that happened, it would have been nothing short of a personal calamity. I had grown weary of eight days sleeping a millimeter from the earth and chanced for a motel room.

I walked in to the Garberville motel and asked them to run my credit card for a night. The gentleman ran the card and it was accepted. I could have a full shower, a mattress that didn't bruise my hips like the earth did. I was very excited. The only real consequence of going over the limit on my credit was a slightly higher percentage, but it really wasn't all that bad, or different. I felt like this town had work for me and I was ready for it. It was a good thing too; I only had one or two aces up my sleeve. I had to make this happen now.

My room had two beds. I didn't know what to do with myself, so I did what anyone celebrating would do, I opened my bottle of three-dollar wine and smoked a nugget of Tahoe. I grew to enjoy the taste though I traditionally didn't really care for weed. I drifted off to sleep dreaming of rows of weed for me to earn money from. When I woke in the morning I decided to milk the hotel room for all it was worth and stay till exactly the check out time. I still had my cardboard sign and went to the grocery store to see if I could get work from a grower. The town only had two grocery stores, one of which was a small, all-organic store. I opted for the big one.

All of my socks were dirty and stinky socks are an unbearable smell in a small tent, so I used some of the money Zeb had wired me to do laundry. I washed everything and used the time waiting to catch up on some reading. Some goofy dude who looked like a poor man's Ricky Gervais was talking way too loud, making comments like, "what do homeless people do all day, just smoke cigarettes?" Nobody answered. He tried on a number of occasions to start a conversation with me, but I made a point to keep my answers terse. He was too dim to notice my tactic and persisted a couple times more. I just ignored him entirely. He stood in front of a message board where a photo of a runaway teen was posted. "Why would a vain girl want to be homeless on purpose?" In my head, I replied, "because you dumb fuck, maybe her dad was beating her? Maybe she had meth heads for parents, maybe you don't know what she was going through and should shut the fuck up". I don't normally speak this way out loud to people, favoring instead a more pleasant reputation, but make no mistake; I have a barrel of savage insults at the ready for anyone shrill enough to elicit my wrath.

Guessing it to be a good spot with maximum traffic, I hung out in front of the grocery store for several hours. I relocated for a bit when I saw that there were officers hassling the local homeless people. I didn't look all that homeless, so I was in the clear. Any time I saw somebody that might not like my solicitation for trim work, I just flipped my sign to say "Free Tarot Readings". I bumped into a fellow that I kept bumping into, Weezy. He had spoken to me the day before about getting a hotel room and cramming it with six people. He was drunk all day, every day, but not in an impolite fashion. We bumped into each other so much that he and his crew started to call me their stalker.

I got hungry and picked up a potpie from the grocery store's deli. As I stood in line a chubby dude with a sneaky look struck up a conversation with me. I had my cardboard sign in plain sight and he asked me what I was doing in town. I'm here looking for work, I said as I made the scissors motion with my fingers. "Oh, you are looking for work? We got work if you want". Hell yeah, I'm all for it. I'll be outside eating my potpie. We can talk out there. Just as agreed, we met outside and the dude took down my phone number. "I'll get a hold of you later on tonight and we'll put you to work". I was thrilled at the thought of not having to ask for money or help from anyone else. I went to the tiny park a couple blocks away and just sat and enjoyed the sun as it began to set. I tried not to obsess about when the dude was gonna call, or if he was gonna forget. I just didn't know.

After sitting for about two hours at the park, I walked over to a third-rate Italian eatery, which was about as Italian as a didgeridoo. I got a cup of coffee and posted up outside with my sign placed prominently beside me. Chubby dude's partner came skating by and told me they weren't gonna do any work tonight, but that they would contact me the next day. At this point it was already dark and I hadn't planned on where I would sleep. I got on the R6 and made my way to the Benbow Golf Course and Campground, about five miles from Garberville. I once again used the maxed credit

Beating a Pot & Singing

card to pay for my thirty-five dollar tent site. As I set up I noticed that Weezy, his girlfriend, and his travel companion were two spots away from me. I shone my light over my face in the dark and Weezy yelled, "Hey, stalker!" Weezy popped over and told me to come hang out with them once I had finished setting up my tent. I did just that and offered some of my weed for sharing.

"So what's the deal with your bike, we were all joking that you were a cop because you look so clean cut". I showed them a google search of me to prove to them that I was indeed not a cop, but a writer on psychedelics and consciousness. They were just busting my balls. I opened up a bottle of three-dollar wine and shared a little while Weezy played his guitar.

It was 7:30 when I got in to the campgrounds and by 8:30 we were all a bit trashed. Weezy suggested we get more to drink back at the front desk mini-store. I picked up a bottle of Happy Camper white wine; for ten bucks it was a remarkable bargain with a rich buttery flavor that gave Chalk Hill a run for its money at a much lower price. As Weezy drove us back to the site after getting more booze, he told me about how much he loved his girl and how he wanted to clean up his drinking at some point. I just nodded and agreed that it sounded like a good plan.

We got back and sang a jumbled rendition of Highwaymen: "I was a sailor, I was born upon the tide. With the sea I did abide, I sailed a schooner round the horn of Mexico. I fell or something fucking mainsail in a blow. And when the bleh fell off they said that I got killed, but I am living still". We killed it at the end with Johnny Cash in his starship: "I'll fly a starship across the universe divine, and when I reach the other side, I'll find a place to rest my spirit where I can. Perhaps I may become a highwayman again, or I may simply be a single drop of rain, but I will remain. I'll be back again and again and again". Weezy showed me all the autographs on his guitar, not a single one of them genuine. He described them as he pointed them out, "Here's Johnny Carson, here's John Hancock, here's Bill Cosby, here's Barack Obama, but I crossed him out because I'm no longer in agreement with his foreign policy". At this point I was pretty stoned and laughed hard at his delivery. His voice was like cinnamon sandpaper and he could have easily been a stand-in for Treebeard from *Lord of the Rings*.

He talked about how much he loved the road, meeting new people and seeing so many rare wonders that everyone else passes without notice. I understood the virtue of living on the road, hitching, living under the radar as much as possible. More people were forced into this life day by day, but to see somebody who lived it by choice and hearing the stories they told made it perfectly clear that there was a gnostic virtue embedded in the life. I again thought of the Cathar perfecti and their cashless travels. It made me wonder why miracles

Beating a Pot & Singing

didn't happen as often in the paper-chasing life that most people call normal. Perhaps it had to do with a dimming of one's perception, a kind of defense mechanism that allowed everyone to cope with a shitty job, a shitty relationship, a house full of shit they didn't need. It made a lot more sense to me than living a bloated life in suburban hell.

I woke up with a prominent hangover and began to gather my things. My tarot reading was so horrible that I did a second one, which was also horrible. I planned on the day being uneventful. Weezy's gang was awake, and I complained about my head as I ate my peanut butter sandwich. We agreed to meet up in town since it was so small that meeting up was inevitable anyway. I sat at the Italian shop again and drank a coffee while displaying my work sign. The chubby fella from the grocery store showed up and told me he would have work "tonight for sure" and reassured me that he would contact me. I agreed and opted to just relax and let life do its thing for a while. I didn't have enough money for camping again, but I had made it this far somehow, so I decided to remain free of worry. No connections to work yet, but it was gonna happen. It's why I came up here, to restart. Nobody said it was going to be easy, many people thought it was insane to even try, but here I was in a one-horse town looking to make a mint in weed if I could just find a farmer with work.

When I got back into town I went to the park, not really knowing what else to do. I got a message from Baby Jesus saying that he was in town and wanted to meet up. He was with a bunch of dudes that looked pretty scruffy. There were two that clearly didn't look as road worn as the others, but the group was a bit suspect in appearance. The grocery store had posted a sign that stated anyone with a backpack was not allowed to come inside, just one more conspicuous slight to out-of-towners. Even worse was the swelling rumor that there was a band of rednecks going around at night, beating up travelers with baseball bats. This news sent fear into the heart of every single traveler trying to make some money in town and was all the encouragement I needed to try to find shelter anywhere but in town. Baby Jesus's crew was the ticket. Since I stayed with Weezy the night before at the Benbow campsite, I knew it was a decent place. We established a group discount there and made our way to Benbow before it got dark because one of the drivers had a busted up car with two broken headlights.

We set up camp and settled in for the night. The group of guys had swelled to seven people. We all drank beer and wine and rambled on about consciousness. I offered my weed for smoking since I didn't smoke all that much and had plenty. We were all cooking food with a portable stove and it looked a bit like a bunch of dwarves making merry. Everyone was dirty and rough around the edges, but this belied their goodwill and generosity. By the time I went to bed, I had done everyone's tarot readings and was spent.

Chapter 9

WHEN I WOKE, MY ENTIRE WEED SUPPLY had been smoked and I didn't really mind all that much. My pitch in for the camp though had drained my account down to three dollars. I felt quite sure that today was the day that I needed to reach out to Betty and do some reparations and allow her to have her say about our split. I rode out to the Redwoods and sent her a message to call me. She called and we talked about our victories and failures as a couple, most of which we agreed about. Hearing her voice after two weeks was heartbreaking. I knew that our split would have to have some measure of pain, but I had heard stories from friends that she had been laid out on the floor for days on end, lamenting and sobbing after I was gone. The weight of freedom can crush bones and I could not escape the fact that I had crushed Betty. After an hour of conversation though, we had come back to peaceable terms. Her voice and mine both quivered with a thick sadness, the kind where you weren't sure if you were winning or losing, you just felt bad. I hadn't left to run away from her, but rather needed the space up to this point to get my feet under me, to just understand myself and where I stood after such a long period of time in which we were too close, too in each other's faces and too involved with the drudgeries of life to focus on the things we really wanted. The kind of sadness we both felt hung heavy like a sack of pennies in our guts, a feeling I never want to feel again. Her parting words to me floated out like haunted souls into the vast forest in which I stood, "I'm just so sorry, I'm sorry for everything". "Me too", I whimpered back. We ended our conversation wishing each other good luck on the next leg of our journey and said goodbye, promising not to try to hurt each other, but to support our separate paths.

I felt this conversation was the breakthrough that I needed, that perhaps this was the way it needed to be in order for me to move forward and for her as well. I got back on my bike and went to find Baby Jesus. When I got into town I bumped into Baby Jesus at the grocery store and he ran in and bought me peanut butter and more bread. "I think I've just got work with this hot Spanish chick, I'll see you later!" I ate some of the new food and walked to my bike. I didn't know what to do so I went to the fancier store and bought some bread. When I stepped out of the store, I saw Jesus with the Spanish girl and decided to give them

Beating a Pot & Singing

some space. I just walked around for a while to kill time, but the vibe in town was really menacing. If you had a backpack on, people assumed you were traveling and that you were up to no good, and I began to really notice the eyes on me. Everywhere I went I was on the R6, and people started to take note. This wasn't something I wanted, especially with rumors of a redneck goon squad on the loose. I came back to the park and walked up to Baby Jesus and his new lady friend. She was doing a tarot reading in a manner I was unfamiliar with; all major arcana mixed and read in sequence as a kind of story line of events. Jesus started talking shit about how Encarna was a much better reader than I, but I knew he was just doing this to impress her. Encarna was a slender, angel-faced gypsy with dark and brooding features that warned of fire, but also welcomed with warmth. She offered to do a reading for me. I sat down and did my best to just let go of all feelings and thoughts. She began to read the full-length spread.

"I can see that you have a love that has ended, this is painful, but it is good. It looks like your mother wants to have control over the things you do, but you are not giving in to her will and it makes her frustrated. Your father is a good man, a pillar in your life, but he too wants to have control on your life, but he uses kindness. He means well, but you must go on your own path, you are no longer a child and have to make your own choices. You are on a journey from being a hermit, to being a magician, somebody who can shine the light of a star from your lantern. If you are able to trust your intuition and keep going, you will become a good light for others. The light comes from your wisdom and your ideas. This is a good journey you are on because you have torn down many old things to make way for the new. Keep going and don't be afraid to trust your own judgment".

I couldn't believe how spot-on the reading was and thanked Encarna for her work. Not too far off, a woman sat and played her guitar, the song was familiar to me from the day just before, "I was a highwayman, along the coach roads I did ride with sword and pistol by my side. Many a young maid lost her bobbles to my trade; many a young man shed his lifeblood on my blade. The bastards hung me in the spring of twenty-five, but I am still alive". As dusk began to fall we went to the Italian deli and Baby Jesus bought me a salmon burger. Thanks, Baby Jesus, I exclaimed as he once again saved me from hunger. I told him about my secret camping spot and we agreed to sleep there that night. Encarna had been picked up on by many dudes in the area with promises of work. We miscreants were still without and she stayed with us until ten PM when we all set off to bed. Baby Jesus couldn't fit on my bike with all of his gear and mine, so he hitched a ride with Encarna's driver. I rode ahead to the spot and dropped off all of my gear. When I got back, Baby Jesus was at the Redway grocery store and I walked him to where my

Beating a Pot & Singing

bike was. I told him that he still had a mile and a half to walk and he agreed to get started.

The night was pitch black and somewhat cold. I rode the bike back up to Baby Jesus and threw him on the back now that I didn't have extra gear to lug. He didn't have a helmet, but I rode him down the hill and around the curves, across a bridge and just past the Humboldt Park and cut my engine, coasting in neutral between the wooden posts intended to keep cars out. Baby Jesus got off and I showed him the area, all the while being cautious about giving away our presence to anyone who might be nearby. I coasted the bike down around to the hidden spot obscured by the road. This was the same spot that I had been spooked at on the first night that I stayed in town, but with Baby Jesus with me, I felt much better about giving it a try. "Aww man, this is a great spot", Jesus exclaimed. Let's set up behind that log by the river. We unraveled all of our gear and set up for the night. With a flashlight in my mouth I rolled the bike into place and set it down. The kickstand gave in just moments after I dismounted and the bike took a spill. The ground was too soft and the angle too hard. I hefted the bike back upright and checked it for damage. Nothing.

I set the bike up on harder ground with a piece of wood under the kickstand for good measure. Feeling like it was safely tucked away, we settled in for the night and I wrapped up in my tarp instead of setting up my two-person tent, which at this point was beginning to really annoy me. As we began to make camp, Jesus asked me if I had dropped my trimming sheers and handed them to me. No, I replied, but felt confused because my sheers were exactly the same as these new ones. I felt like a hobbit discovering a cache of swords, like my journey had been confirmed. This night was the first night in my life that I had slept under the stars as an adult in a guerilla environment. The land itself appeared to be public property, but lacked any signage about not being able to camp there. I fell asleep with little effort after Baby Jesus and I talked. When we woke in the morning, we planned to stand in front of the grocery store in Redway instead of going back to Garbageville. Things felt increasingly hostile there and we needed a change of scenery.

We packed up early in the morning and I made my way on the motorcycle ahead of Baby Jesus who unfortunately had to walk up the hill with all his shit. Two of my books had sold a month before, and I discovered a deposit of ten dollars in my account. I used the money to buy breakfast sandwiches and coffee for Jesus and I. As we stood outside in the early morning cold, a blond-haired viking of a man walked past us. A few moments later he came out with a coffee and greeted us. "So are you guys out here for what we're out here for?" Yeah, man, we're here to find some work. "My name's Cal, it's nice to meet you guys. I see you've got a tarot deck, can you do readings?" Yeah, I can

Beating a Pot & Singing

do one for you if you want, I replied. "That would be great". I divvied out his cards and like many others he seemed impressed about the reading.

He told us that there was a community meal at noon and we should go and get some eats. We stood around and assessed which ones entering the store were growers or not. It was a fun game until a grocery store clerk told us to leave. I was going to make a stink about how they wanted our money just fine, but as soon as the money exchanged hands they wanted us to stop existing again. It was infuriating to me that this was the way business was done in this area. Noon had arrived and Baby Jesus decided to head back to Garberville and meet up with Encarna and maybe score some work on her coattails. I went to the lunch with Cal. We stood waiting for the doors to open and a large group began to amass. It was clear that there was a need for people to get food. My brother called to check in and gave me some consolation that he was enjoying hearing about my journey and asked if I needed help. I told him I was down to zero cash and he offered to wire me fifty bucks. I took the offer and settled in for the community meal.

As I looked for a place to sit, a group of four gutter punks invited me in. Just as I got settled, a larger woman with mostly silver teeth came to say hi and ask how we were doing. The rumors of the goon squad had gotten all over and she told us more. A couple of years ago, a local went across the street over there and bashed in a traveler's head. He murdered him while he was asleep. He got three years in prison and they just let him out. The most shocking part of this is that the community was split over the attack; some defended it while others were horrified. The police would not allow a wreath or flowers to be placed at the site of the murder. It's like they didn't even want to acknowledge that it ever happened, but now somebody is dead and this guy is free again.

This story didn't do anything to make me feel better about the goon squad, who obviously had partial support from the community. I had trouble eating the rest of my food, knowing that this community misused their workers so harshly. The lady continued. "Our finances go up anywhere from 150 to 300 percent during September, October, and November, and people are making money hand over fist, yet we can't provide a proper bathroom, or place for people to camp at. It's disgusting to me".

I got on the R6 and made my way back to Garberville to meet with Jesus and Encarna. They were in the park doing Yoga and I sat beside them just enjoying the sunshine and the breeze. We sat there quietly and peacefully, eventually playing a little bass ukulele and simply enjoying the day. Without notice a woman with a dog came up behind us and snapped pictures of us on her phone. I turned around and said, hi. She replied, "why don't you dirty people go out and get real jobs instead of stinking up this town with your shit and all

Beating a Pot & Singing

your garbage. You're in a park and children can't play while you are here". I told her that we were just hanging out in a park in America, a right that we still had. She said we were disgusting humans and that she was going to call the sheriff. Ironically, the only person breaking the law was her. Behind her there stood a sign that said, "No dogs allowed". All of this hate really came down hard and depressed me. I was clean and well-kept, as were Jesus and Encarna, but the people of the town were lashing out unreasonably. People like that lady wished for the goon squad to come and beat us into a coma. She drooled and masturbated to the images of the dead kid, murdered by the redneck batting club. Her hate filled the whole park with darkness.

A rage welled up inside of me that I hadn't felt in a long time, a disgust at the lack of understanding, the lack of courtesy, the unprovoked attacks and verbal abuse. I wondered what fucking job she had, what fucking money she made. Did she benefit from the weed business? Of course she did, but she wanted to bite the hand that feeds, to get her service then hope we disappeared, she wanted free people to not exist, because we represented a freedom that she would never know, to let your intuition guide you and bask in the sunlight of a park, free of hate. What a sad life she must have had to lash out like that at regular people. She complained of shit in the streets, but there wasn't a single public toilet in the whole town.

We were offered a spot in Cal's camper in Redway and decided to give it a try. Once again, I rode off and Baby Jesus walked the four miles back. We set all of our stuff inside the camper and I prepared a meal for everyone. The scenario Cal had described was far from the reality that we observed as we boarded. Cal claimed that he had dishes and a stove, which was true. What he had left out was that the stove was covered in garbage and all the dishes were dirty. With half a dozen stoned vagrants in close quarters taking bong rips using a propane torch, I fashioned quite a spectacular zucchini and broccoli dish. The camper was one of the most third world country looking scenarios I had come across, making the woods seem like a better option if not for the possibility of insulting our gracious hosts. After my finely crafted meal, Baby Jesus and I headed to a bar that was supposedly full of growers taking a little break for beer. When we got in, our friend Ben was there and was noticeably tanked. It was a relief because we hadn't heard from him for a while. Jesus kindly bought me a beer and we played some pool. Before we knew it, it was 12:30 and we made our way back to Cal's camper. Everyone was asleep and we piled in. Jesus took a spot under the front bunk, which was occupied by two of the drifter kids, one of which was a pregnant nineteen year old. I slept on the camper floor and shared the tight space with one of the drifter's dogs who laid its head between my legs.

Beating a Pot & Singing

It wasn't long before the pregnant teen that slept on the bench above me began to flop her arm onto me in her sleep. It was like being randomly slapped. At one point in the night when I had turned to face in her direction, she gave me a punch to the face. She got my forehead, so it wasn't really all that painful, but it was one of the more uneasy nights of sleep I've ever had. As soon as daybreak came, I quietly got out of there and made my way out to Garberville.

Baby Jesus had hitched a ride with a new job seeker and offered to buy me a coffee at the local greasy spoon. I abstained from any food, except for what was offered. I was officially down to ninety-five cents in my bank account and maxed on my credit card. I ate the scraps like a dog and was thankful. The same small park that had hosted the demon woman from the day before had been transformed into a farmers market. I used the opportunity to give people some tarot readings and earned enough cash to buy myself lunch. One woman seemed so inspired by my reading that she gave me a twenty dollar bill, which might as well have been a million in my hungry mind. After the market had died down, Baby Jesus met up with me where I was sitting and writing, he got me a coffee and we chatted about what we were going to do for the night. We had both agreed that Cal's camper was out of the question and opted for our secret spot in the woods.

We sat there till well after nightfall and I went on ahead to set up camp while Jesus worked on a ride, or a walk to the spot. I coasted into the hiding spot silently as I had done before and crept the bike down to the camping spot. It was dark, cold, and scary alone, but having slept there the night before last, I felt better about it. I put my folding knife in my teeth as I lay there waiting for Baby Jesus to arrive. I laid there for hours watching the lights of the passing cars dance across the trees, making a play of light and shadow that was mysterious and beautiful. I dozed off with my knife clutched in my hand and awoke at ten PM and texted Jesus; he had stopped for a glass of wine with some women he had met. Jesus never came and I realized that I would be alone in the dark heart of the forest. It was the devil's night and yet it came and went without incident.

When I awoke and returned to town Baby Jesus and I sat down for a coffee. He made fun of me as I described being fearful in the forest alone, while proceeding to gloat about staying up and smoking weed and drinking with a bunch of foreign girls. We both felt good, though, and I didn't take the ribbing personally. As Jesus attested to the virtues of Yogic practice, his phone rang and he stopped and smiled. We had been hired.

Chapter 10

IT WAS A VERY LONG DRIVE FOLLOWING OUR new employer to the work site. We were hours from Garberville, way up north past Arcata and deep into the hills. The road was unlike anything I had ever encountered on a motorcycle, perhaps even in a car. There were potholes everywhere, gravel-infested corners on downward slopes, single-lane sections with fifty-foot death drops and no guard rails. I struggled to keep up with our employer as I followed along, doing my best to balance caution and speed. It was a difficult task. As the road climbed higher the view became breathtaking and I understood why Northern California was so priceless. A man could happily lose himself here and never be seen again, settling in on some plot of land with a little solar power, a stream, and a couple weed plants to keep things exciting. It made me long to have a piece of land of my own, something I could establish for generations to come for my son and daughter.

My mind jumped between the excitement of getting work and the thrill of opening up the R6 on the twisty roads. As the road narrowed I came to a long and meandering corridor of large trees that arched high over the road. As the vehicle in front of me led the way, the leaves of the trees fell like rusted rainbow beams. It was as if I had won a great victory in some foreign land and this was my ticker tape parade. Even nature herself was celebrating, showering me with her praise as the wind picked up the leaves and swirled them around before me. And it was indeed a great victory, I didn't look like these people, I didn't sound like them, but I was just like them in my effort to try something different from what I had always done, and Goddammit, I did it! After three quarters of a year without work, I was employed. On many occasions during the long and winding ride, I encountered cattle on the road and deer casting aloft, nearly missing me at one point. I saw the wonders of life unfolding before me like they had been waiting all my life to greet me in this moment. Though I was tearing along the road, I was completely still on the inside, a peace that came from a Hail Mary successfully executed.

When I arrived on the scene, the road before me got very steep and rocky, making it difficult for my tight suspension to deal with, so I did my best to have fun with it and skidded my back brake from time to time, just for kicks. When I finally parked, I walked out into a field that had dozens

Beating a Pot & Singing

of lovely pot plants still growing and an overpowering smell of fresh weed. In all my days, I never thought I would find myself in a place like this and yet, here I was, miracle after miracle leading me right here. I observed other trimmers that were hard at work and watched how they did it so that I could get off to a good start. Night came quickly and I set up my tent and prepared for a good night's rest because morning and the first day's work would come soon. I took a hit of a dark colored strain that had been growing there and called it a night.

When I awoke, the rest of the group had only partially gathered groggily for coffee. The boss arrived with a tub full of weed on the branch. She had given us the smallest ones that she had, obviously as a test to see if we would whine and moan, or just shut up and do the work. Baby Jesus and I sat apart from the rest of the group so that we could just zen out and see if we could get up to a pound, which was the daily goal. Within three days, I had gotten up to a pound per day of perfectly trimmed weed, a feat that required anywhere between nine and eleven hours of work, at least for me.

Before I knew it, day after day unfolded and I drifted between dreams of building pyramids in the California desert and fantasies about working toward my doctorate. There were some big changes that had already occurred from what I now saw as my previous life. For one thing I had been drinking myself to sleep for years and averaged two bottles of wine per night. Here in the wilderness there was not much in the way of drink and so the set of symptoms that come with heavy drinking also faded. I didn't snore horribly, I didn't have rampant thirst, I didn't wake up at four AM unable to return to sleep till well after I should have been up. I also didn't take into account that the average bottle of wine is eleven hundred calories and at two bottles per night, I was throwing in about three thousand calories in just before bed, since I'd no doubt get hungry and eat something just before sleep as well. I did smoke the weed that was so abundantly available, though in small amounts, and I found that my sleep was deep and abundant without the horrendous challenge of a hangover that lasted half the day. I admit this with a bit of embarrassment, but that's how it was and what I had become. Without my nightly blanket of drink, the pounds started falling off me rapidly and by the time I had been there two weeks, I had already lost ten pounds.

This didn't mean the rest of the group wasn't partying; in fact only Baby Jesus and I refrained most nights. One girl in the group that I had met before down in town, the one who wanted to be Keroac's lover, was clearly the kind of person who should not be drinking. She drank anything and everything available long after everyone else had stopped. In the firelight I could see in her slanted and swaying face the look of a woman twenty years down the road, haggard and weary, beaten

Beating a Pot & Singing

and trashed to unrecognizable levels. I saw this in her young, beautiful face and thought about how I might look when I was this shit faced.

Baby Jesus and I still kept mostly to ourselves. He was an excellent verbal sparring partner and we listened to podcast after podcast of interesting material, from public radio segments to New Age gurus. He and I were two sides of the same coin, new blood bringing further life into the consciousness community. Ben, too, was an excellent person to talk to, though he was often occupied with Pinky, or the office politics of the weed farm. Baby Jesus and I were the odd men out, the latecomers to the tribe, and though Jesus had been with the crew before, his more assertive spiritual overtones dampened the party atmosphere that had been the staple of the group before our arrival. It soon became apparent that we would work for our boss and the rest of the group would work for theirs. So, though we worked in the same area, we were on different teams.

This was fine with me, I was just happy to have finally found some work, but strain to strain, the stuff we worked on was twice as hard to trim as the stuff the other guys had, which ended up making a fifty to one hundred dollar difference in our wages despite the same amount of time being put in. Trimming weed is an art form all of its own. Each bud you trim must look flawless to the buyer at the shop and must look rounded, free of rootlike 'crows feet' crowding around the base of the bud. When you really got going in cleaning up the buds, it became its own zen ritual where hours upon hours would go by without making much more than the sound of trim scissors flick-flick-flicking away. The smell of weed disappeared unless you put your nose right to it, but it was everywhere and when people left and came back to camp, they would always comment on the deep, rich smell of the weed farm. Lost in the zen of this seemingly endless labor, Jesus and I sat across from each other like two gurus teaching the other half of the lesson.

Chapter 11

AFTER BEING SECLUDED IN THE DENSELY forested Northern California hills on a farm for two weeks, I needed a break, and since I had just gotten paid fifteen hundred dollars, it felt like I had earned a little comfort. I headed down the long roads back to what passed for civilization and settled into the cheapest hotel between the two adjacent towns. There was a bar across the street and since I had been so well behaved, I figured letting loose a bit wouldn't be so bad. I shaved my face after accruing a monumentally burly beard over the last month, figuring it may increase my chances of getting laid, or at the very least talking to something pretty. The hotel was nothing to speak of, but the water was hot and the shower worked and there was decent internet service. I made my first social media update in weeks: *Civilization is a term I loosely use for where I am at the moment, but it's good to have a hot shower and a cold beer on the way.*

I drank two Coors Lights and took a hit of the purple weed I had and ventured over to the bar. The way my mind works, I had imagined some kind of Budweiser cabin party waiting for me there, but that of course was not the case. The bar was full of scruffy dudes playing pool and sharking the three or four not pretty girls that made up the feminine aspect of the bar. After two drinks more those girls got prettier, but I had no motivation to do anything other than watch. The theater of provincial mating was ready and the curtains were drawn back to reveal bad dancing, bad teeth, bad country music, and sketchy situations. The bar was the common denominator between the rednecks, the hippies, and the gutter punks who all peopled the area and the dynamic was friendly, but had a feel like it could take a turn at any time. I pretty much drank alone except for some hellos between travelers and workers I had recognized. If you were between these two towns for more than a day hanging out, you'd easily recognize and be recognized. I left an hour before closing time and got into bed. Out of habit, I had put my sleeping bag on top of the hotel bed and slept inside of it. Somehow that felt better, safer. It had been a very long time since I had felt free to spend my own money, or really do anything with it. For years and years, I had virtually handed my paychecks over to Betty voluntarily, ensuring that all our bills would be paid on time. The idea of spending much of anything on myself was pretty foreign, at least

Beating a Pot & Singing

buying something for myself and not getting hell for it when I got home.

I spent another day doing laundry at the local spot and enjoying comforts like ice and wine and tacos. The food at the campsite was minimalist, rice, beans, more rice, more beans, occasional cheese, chili, and so on. I had to ride an hour out of the way to my bank to make necessary payments on bills that were either past due, or about to be. After all was said and done, eleven hundred dollars had gone away. Even after all I had accomplished, it was still like treading water, but at least I was making it, at least I was working after such a long dry spell. After spending another two hundred and thirty dollars on the hotel stays and some nicer food and drink items, I was pretty much at zero again. Baby Jesus had given me his phone and instructed me to text a few people and let them know he was doing well. He also had me try to get a hold of a friend of his, Dani. Dani was a yoga guru girl as well, and was driving out to Cali from the East Coast to find work. Up to this point, Baby Jesus had only just recently found work as I had. I had to relay the message to Dani that she needed to wait. I sent the message before I got to a place where the reception vanished and finished the long ride back to the encampment.

When I returned, it seemed that the tone of our small trim village had taken a turn for the worse; whispering and conspiring became pervasive. I had a good ten years on virtually everyone there except for my boss who only was around in the morning and for a moment at night, so I was pretty reticent to be involved in any of their "drug dealer" nonsense. I was simply there to work. The other team that we worked side by side with decided to move along to a house the growers owned in a town a couple hours away, so everyone filtered out over the next day or two, leaving just Baby Jesus and I. This suited me just fine, though I did miss Ben's company.

A couple of days later, a Canadian fellow and his extremely attractive girlfriend showed up to work there for a few days, but while they were there, they left their mark. The dude was blonde and often lived and worked without his shirt on, showing his bad tattoos and dangly *Star Wars*-style "Padewan" rat tail braid. He would grill me at night over the campfire about *Reality Sandwich*, told me his Burning Man story about the psychedelic writer, David Foolsgold, being a phony. He also proclaimed the true way to do magic and shared other opinionated rants. He seemed nice enough, but something about the situation was disjointed. He seemed to have a control over his girlfriend that was unsettling; not bad, or abusive, but when he told her what to do, she did it immediately, like a master to a servant. He, the real life Padewan, decided that when he got paid, he was going to buy an "authentic" Jedi sword of some sort that used real laser light, or something to that effect. I wasn't very interested, but

Beating a Pot & Singing

he seemed quite ecstatic about it. When he told our boss about it, our boss just looked at us all like we were crazy.

Surprisingly, the weather was still hot and we all decided to go down to the creek where there was a watering hole. The route to the creek required a rope climb down into a ravine and a very steep walk down loose gravel. At one point, our water reservoir had run out and not refilled since the team that left had the water pump, so now we were forced up and down this precarious roped cliff with our daily ration of water from the creek. The creek served as a great place to relax though, so we decided to go for a dip. In classic Baby Jesus fashion, he clamored down the hill barefoot and of course the Padewan was shirtless. When we got to the watering hole, Padewan jumped right in and immediately turned bright red. The water was ice cold and I could barely stand just dangling my feet in the water. But in his own weird tough-guy way, he refused a towel to dry off with when he got out. We all just sat in the shade enjoying a view other than that of the campsite, which became just like any other jobsite; not something you always want to spend your time at. A few more days went on without incident, the Canadian couple left and another week rolled by. I was relieved, because being without any intimacy for so long, it was hard watching Padewan fawn over his archetypally vestal hippie girlfriend with her long, brown, feathered hair, flowy patterned dresses, sparkling emerald eyes, and lithe form. It was one of those weird situations where the guy talked for his girl like the jerky bad guys in films from the 80s used to. In fact, I'm not sure she said more than a handful of sentences.

We were edging closer and closer to mid-November and the weather got progressively colder, becoming quite unbearable. It was cold, but not wet, something I was very thankful for as the mix would have been bad news considering I was ill-equipped for winter camping. So when the time came to return to civilization, I had a big list of items I needed to get. When I made it to town, I picked up a new sweatshirt, a fleece sleeping bag liner that increased the warmth of my present sleeping bag, a new stocking cap for my head, new boots, some lighters, and more food. I was only planning to stay one night in town, but my boss said the flow was slow, so stay another day. I did and when it was time for me to come back, misfortune struck. Forest fires were common and it had been a very dry year. The hills were on fire and the only road back to camp was literally in the center of the fire zone. As I pulled to the police barricade on the road, the officer said the road was so hot that the painted dividing line was on fire. So I had little choice but to spend more money and stick around town.

I rode between the two towns out of sheer boredom and at one point passed a river, where to my surprise a helicopter was drawing water to fight

Beating a Pot & Singing

the fire with. It was comforting, but surreal to see a helicopter popping up out of a river valley just beside the road with a massive water carriage beneath it. Planes were dropping a red powder on the fires as the helicopter made its runs to and from the river to fight the fire. As evening came, the hills glowed above the city like fiery worms crawling along the ridges. It was an eerie kind of beautiful that only those who have seen can fully appreciate.

Desperate for interaction, I went to the grocery store and milled around for a bit. Having nothing but my loneliness, I returned to the hotel room. It wasn't until another uneventful day later that the road was reopened, having been deemed safe to pass through, and as I rode the R6 through the hills, everything blackened and charred. It looked like a warzone. When I returned to camp, Baby Jesus had gotten word from Dani that she was in town, so he headed out to get her with my boss. I was left there to work on my own for the next two days while Baby Jesus had his break and when Jesus returned with Dani, I was delighted to see that she was super nice and friendly.

It had only rained once, but it was cold, violent and miserable, so we put it to a vote and I was commissioned to improve the tent situation. There were dozens of yards of industrial plastic used to cover greenhouses, so I used it to wrap, under, over and round our tents, essentially turning them into cocoons. Mine had an entryway, which I was quite proud of, and all of it would soon be put to the test as the winter winds and snows began to fall.

This was what I dreaded since my only vehicle was a motorcycle intended for smooth, flat racetracks. I could easily be stranded until the snow cleared. No matter what I did, the volume I produced each day wasn't enough; we were undersupplied with weed and what we did have was hard to trim, so the incentive to stay got less and less, especially considering that there was now snow on the ground and I had frozen boots every day. The days had grown miserably cold without any real escape except to double and triple up our coats with extra shirts underneath, sleeping wrapped in sleeping bags and plastic. It was a frozen mess. Our drinking water was frozen, our coffee press had frozen solid, the outdoor makeshift toilet was covered in ice. To make matters worse, Dani had gotten poison ivy and was working in that condition. It became clear that our time in the hills was coming to an end.

Chapter 12

AT THIS POINT, BABY JESUS HAD BEEN MY best companion since I left LA, and now I was watching him leave with his girl. We said hug-filled goodbyes and they went on to their own new set of adventures as a couple, having established a deeper bond with one another as they lived and worked together. As for me, I was still very alone and wondering how in the fuck I was going to get off the mountain. It was now early December and I stayed a few more days in the empty camp hoping the roads would be better soon. My boss checked the roads daily for me to see if they might be passable. Finally the time came where my boss said the roads looked "mostly clear". For me, that was all I needed to hear.

My poor bike was covered in ice for days on end, and it took some time for it to warm up. I had moved it before the first snow into a shelter that was being used to dry out the weed. Before I could even get to the road, I would have to travel three quarters of a mile through foot-deep untouched snow up a hill. Trying to do this with my motorcycle alone, packed with a fully loaded bike and a fifty-pound backpack was simply impossible. My boss pulled her quad up to my bike and wrapped a car-towing strap around the front forks of my bike. In what I can only characterize as the most brilliant and dangerous backwoods towing job I've ever come across, we inched up the hill, essentially being dragged and sledded by my boss riding in reverse. Miraculously, I made it to the top and said goodbye to my kind employer.

As I waved goodbye, she said that the road I was accustomed to was still snowbound and not even passable by 4x4 truck, so I had to take a road I had not tried before. I turned on to the bare, wet road and drove down around the corner, out of sight from the entrance to the place I had called home for a month and a half. To my utter disbelief, the road before me raised and shone white with compacted snow with only single lines of black where the asphalt was visible. I opted to ride along the line wherever the asphalt was. One hill at a time passed in this manner, sometimes with sections that arched up and over around corners with only compacted snow.

My bike was top heavy with gear and the road was downright deadly. It was only a matter of time before I pushed my luck too hard trying to rally up a steep and iced hill that I first dumped the R6. I can't explain the desperation I felt. Was I stuck? Stranded for good? I knew nobody would be

Beating a Pot & Singing

around to save me and being out in the elements at night would be just as dangerous as riding, so I did everything I could to keep going. I lifted the bike and let it slide backwards on the ice into the ditch that for the most part followed the road the whole way. Using the debris, twigs, and roots as traction, I managed to break free from the steep hill, only to find another, and another, and another waiting for me. It was absolutely exhausting. The trip itself would have taken an hour and a half to get to regular highways, but in these conditions, I had only traveled a handful of miles.

As I made my way down a steep hill riding over the patches of dry asphalt and ice, I saw a long hill up ahead, a good eighth of a mile long with a steeper turn to the left at the ridge. Before attempting to take the hill, I walked up it to assess what was at the top. To my relief, it was a long dry patch. I carefully walked back down the icy hill in my flat-footed cowboy boots and did my best to try to map out where I would ride. There was a dry patch about six feet long that I could get a boost of traction from. Then and there, I had no choice but to try. I found that the magic speed for the bike was eleven miles per hour. At this speed I could dump it without too much risk of personal injury, so as I began my ascent, I put it to fifteen, knowing that my grip would exponentially decrease on the icy slope I climbed. As I made my way up, the bike began to slow to a halt and then slide backwards. With my backpack and gear, I carried about 290 pounds on top of the 413 pound bike. This meant I was now sliding backwards on a compacted ice hill with flat-footed boots trying to hold it all up with my two feet. I was full of terror. By grace, dumb luck, and sheer "what-the-fuck", I was able to bring the bike tenuously to a halt. I stood there in a panic knowing that with even a slight change in weight balance, the whole thing would keep sliding down the hill backwards. It was the ditch to my right, a mere eight feet away, that again was my salvation. I painstakingly inched my way backward with the front brake gently letting out until I was able to put the bike in the ditch. Now I still had that dry patch twenty yards ahead of me and I aimed to find a way up through the ditch. I got off the bike which stood on its own in the deep and skinny ditch, and gathered sticks, rocks, and debris of any kind that would act as traction for the Gnostic Rocket. I laid sticks out like railroad ties for a good ten yards. It now came time to get this fucker up the hill and I went for it.

At first rev, the engine died, not enough juice to keep it from seizing. Second rev took the RPMs to eight-thousand and the speedometer to reading forty miles per hour. I jerked, slid, and lunged with fierce anxiety, using my legs to push along the embankment. I scraped for every inch of forward motion with the bike seizing and screaming back and forth, my right leg pushing off as I went dangerously up. I had gained a certain momentum and rhythm and was determined to make it

Beating a Pot & Singing

work. I bolted the bike to the dry patch and lunged again a long stretch up and thought I could make it to the top so I gave it all I dared to give it. Just then, a large old brown Ford pickup truck came down and around the corner and I had to decide whether to be struck head on, or to dump the bike in front of the truck. I had no choice, but to fall. I had been struggling along for over two hours and had not seen a single vehicle and it just so happened that the first one I saw was the one that nearly took my life and squelched my conquest of the hill from hell.

Without missing a beat, I got up from my crash and walked over to the window of the truck where a surprised woman sat. "How does the road look ahead?" I asked as pleasantly as only a person in shock could ask. "It's worse than this ahead, you need to go back the way you came". I thanked her and without an offer to help, or a word of any further pleasantness, she drove off around my bike as it lay there on its side on the steepest part of the hill just ten yards from the crest where the sunlight had carved through the snow and into the now dirt road. There in my helmet I began to scream, FUUUUUUUUCK! FUCK FUCK FUCK FUCK! FUUUUUUCK! I came to my senses as best I could. I asked myself if this was the part of my story where I sit and cry like a child, or where I do something extraordinary and carry on? I resolved to not be defeated by this goddamn hill, but I needed a moment: I was now freshly wrecked and warned by the brown-trucked harbinger of doom that things would get worse. I lightly limped in my boots to the crest of the hill, took off my pack and just sat there, leaving the bike in the center of that icy road. I sat for fifteen minutes just trying to be still, to be optimistic, to not worry, but I was in serious danger of being stranded overnight in the middle of nowhere.

The bike was closer to the oncoming side of the road than it was to the proper side, but the ditch was shallower and had an okay run to complete the journey to the top. I tried to lift the bike, but in the position it was in, it kept sliding down on its fairing and I could get no grip with my flat-footed boots. I tried again and again, worrying I might throw out my back from the strain. The bike wouldn't budge. I stood back and stared at it, full of frustration and agony, wishing I was somewhere else, wishing I could see my kids, wishing for anything but this; but here I was, not in any other place, and I needed to do something. I walked to the embankment and found a busted tree branch as big as my arm and wedged it underneath the back tire. I resolved that if I could just get the tiniest amount of leverage from the fixed position of the branch, I could prop the bike up and deal with the next issue of making the rest of the way up. With everything I had I was able to lift the bike up enough to wedge my slipping foot and knee under the fallen side of the bike. I had just that moment to adjust my hands' positioning and to prop up

Beating a Pot & Singing

further, and I did. I was relieved to be upright. Having mastered the art of janky backwoods snowbound sportbike salvage, I made quick work of the last ten yards using the ditch method and onto the dirt road I arrived.

I sat and rested for half an hour just staring blankly into the trees. The sun began to fade and I was not close at all to any passable road. I took a walk down the road to see how it looked and to my chagrin saw that it was worse than all roads prior, absolutely impossible to cross. I looked around and saw no suitable place to try to get help; there was no cell service, no nothing. Moment to moment it got colder and I started to wonder if I would be camping up against a tree without protection from the elements. I just sat there watching the sun slowly fall and cast the shadows of the tall trees over me, the gorgeous winter wasteland closing around me like the jaws of a great beast.

Off in the distance I heard a tremendous racket like the sound of falling beams, and for a long time it persisted. Finally up the road came an odd-looking industrial truck. As it effortlessly crested the hill, the jolly driver came to a stop and rolled down his window. "Looks like you're stuck there, friend! Maybe I could load that bike into the truck?" I looked at the truck and saw only a long metal beam too thin to even give a footing for my motorcycle tires. "Yeah, I guess there's no place to put it, huh? Well, gee I wish there was something I could do for you. Do you want a ride into town?"

The thought of leaving the R6 abandoned on a remote country road sounded like a really bad idea in a day full of bad ideas already hatched. "I think I would rather just have you send a tow truck for me. Would you be able to do that when you get to town?" The town was still easily a good hour and a half from our position with the road travel conditions. "Yeah, I'll send them your way". I thanked the driver as he drove off. The idea of rescue put my now fever-pitched mind to ease, that is, for the first two hours that I waited.

The sun had all but dropped out of sight and I was freezing without shelter. Then something extraordinary happened. A flatbed truck with double back axles pulled up with two brawny country boys inside, both pink-faced, chewing tobacco and covered in grime. Without so much as a hello, they got out and assessed how they might load the bike into the bed. They instructed me to ride the bike into the adjoining field that stood a good five feet higher than the road. They backed the bed of the truck to the embankment and I road the bike through the snowy field up to the bed. The two men lifted the bike, wheels and all, into the flatbed, rolled it forward, and strapped it down securely. I hopped in and sat there shoulder to shoulder with them, feeling like a rescued refugee.

The boys explained casually that they pick up stranded people on the back roads all the time. It was just a part of the deal. I told them that I had sent for a tow truck, and they laughed out loud.

Beating a Pot & Singing

"Hah, yeah, there ain't no tow truck that's gonna come on a wild goose chase on a dirt road. The only tow in town is run by this guy in his eighties, who only tows on easy highways, and he goes to bed at eight PM. No, you would have been stuck out there". I expressed my gratitude to the gentlemen and sat and listened to the howl of the wind and the breathtaking sunset that the winter dusk had prepared. Through long s-curves and stretches of icy road, the truck danced and slid around, making its way down, down, down the hills and through the peaks and valleys.

Across a tumultuous-looking bridge we drove, passing a man who looked like Santa, waving cheerily as we drove by. He wasn't waving for help; he was just waving. Once across, we bent and swept up and over till the truck stopped for another man with a dog who needed a lift. "There's no room in the cab, but you can sit in the back if you want". Without a word, the guy placed his dog on the bed and hopped on, wrapping his arm around the strap that tied my bike down. It was in that moment that I stopped feeling sorry for myself. No matter how bad I had it, this guy had it worse, but we were both riding together, this motley assemblage of strangers on a snowy road, partners for a time in a simple shared destiny called making it to town alive. It was dark and frigid and the town only had one hotel. The back passenger pounded on the back window to stop. He hopped off and went on his way. Without much more than a wave we carried on.

They drove me to their house on the only road the town had, propped a ramp against the back of the flatbed and out I went, free to ride the roads that only had black ice. I went straight for the hotel and got a room. They could have charged me five hundred dollars and I would have had no choice but to pay, but lucky for me it was only ninety. There was a corner store next door with a burger joint, and I sat and ate the shitty burger with thanks. I was absolutely filthy, cold, bedraggled and beat to death, wrecked and wind worn, but I was safe. I got in the shower and ran it as hot as I could stand it, trying to wash off the metallic cold that ran to my core. I had the red wine for the inside and the hot water for the outside. I called my brother and told him I was safe. Nobody had heard from me for over a week. I slept hard and heavy and when I awoke, I felt like a new kind of freedom was at hand, until I walked outside.

Chapter 13

THE SUN HAD NOT YET HIT THE SPOT WHERE my bike had been parked, and solid sheets of ice encrusted much of it. I had to break off ice from around the wheels to roll it out into the light. I knew that the melt would take a little bit of time so I rolled to the other end of the parking lot where no shade was to be found, set the R6 back down and made my way over to the burger place that was now serving breakfast. When I walked in, I was the only person there. I ordered bacon and eggs. The seats were badly cushioned, with worn-out, cracked brown vinyl. The décor was patched spackle walls with badly hand-drawn signs about burger and fry combos, warnings about no free refills hanging over the prominently displayed soda fountain, which served as the centerpiece. On the first-generation flat screen, a football game played. I didn't know what day of the week it was; it hadn't mattered for two months and I wasn't about to start caring about a detail like that just yet. The eggs came and were decent, the bacon barely worth mentioning, and the coffee had been on the burner too long. All things considered, though, it might as well have been a fancy breakfast at Four Seasons, because I had made it out of the hills alive. I tipped well.

The town I had made it to was beset on all sides by mountains and there was only one viable option for escape; to take the main road out of town and follow it till I hit the 101, some forty miles away. I asked the woman at the counter who served as the cook, hostess, and server what the conditions were like and she conveyed that cars had been coming and going, indicating they were at least passable. I knew what was considered as passable the day before and took little reassurance from her input. Nevertheless, I made my way to the bike and turned the key and pressed the start button. Nothing happened. A panic came over me, "What if the bike is dead?" I tried again and it chugged to a start. I let her warm up for a good long time before pulling out onto the road. I gassed up at the only station in town and headed down the road. It felt amazing to be at freeway speeds without fear of certain death floating over my head, but soon that glee gave way to a new pensive stature that I would have to take on as the road crept up into the low-lying hills again. The road was clear on the west side of the hills and iced over on the east, so I went back and forth on high alert across thick sheets of ice and onto bare, dry road. The road itself twisted and turned through the hills along-

Beating a Pot & Singing

side a breathtaking river too beautiful to ignore, had I not been riding white knuckles over ice half the time. I stopped to look at the river with its emerald greens, shimmering blues, and dancing torrid rushes of whitecaps overarched by daunting brown hills frosted at their peaks with my beautiful bane of crystalline snow.

I finally made it through the second gauntlet of ice and peril and thought perhaps once I hit 101 the trouble would subside, but as I looked down the highway, I could see strips of ice and ruts of wet asphalt, but the semis and SUVs whizzing down the road were traveling between sixty and seventy miles per hour. This meant the risk of shady spots at highway speed that threatened to take me out at a moments notice. This predicament was exacerbated by the fact that at many points, the highway was one lane each direction, and oncoming traffic was right there at arms length. Semis carrying full loads would rush by and blow the bike easily into a patch of ice. But there I was and I felt I had no choice but to go, so I did. I was hours from San Francisco and I made my way quickly, but cautiously along the breathtaking 101, occasionally pulling by the side of the road to let the caravan of aggressive vehicles pass me before following the pack. Eventually the road cleared, and I only had to deal with the cold as I rode along the highway.

Once again I had to make payments and once again, virtually everything I had earned would go away in a heartbeat. I stopped at a café in one of the small towns I passed through and enjoyed an espresso and sparkling water; everything was a miracle in that moment. I looked clearly road worn and had already spent much of the day's light getting through the rougher part of the ride, but I was happy for a moment's respite. I was told the town an hour or so down the road had my bank, so that's where I planned to stop next. I made my deposits and payments and got back on. It was my hope to stay with my old New York friends, Barney and Hillary in San Francisco, but I was soon to find out that things were not as I had imagined. When Betty and I parted ways, people had problems with the way it went down. This is always to be expected, but it never happens the way we want, or the way it should in a perfect world. The reality is that people break up and get together every day, people come and people go, but some make it their business to take sides, place blame, and act as if they had never been in the same position.

I called Barney and checked in. We hadn't talked since our times together in NYC, but he and I were pretty close for a time. Hillary and Betty had become good friends and we often hung out as couples. I asked if they were around in SF and he said he was out of town. Being good friends with both him and Hillary, I messaged her to see if she wanted to meet for coffee when I got in to San Francisico. I messaged, "Hey, it's Gabe, I'll be in SF tonight. Wanna meet for coffee?". She replied, "You're going to be in SF? Cool! I thought you were

Beating a Pot & Singing

in New York!" I responded, "No, I've been in the mountains in NorCal and am riding in on my bike. Stoked to see you!" She replied, "Wait, is this Gabe Mortinson?" and I responded, "Gabe Roberts". I waited twenty minutes for a response, but none would come again. I knew what had happened and later could understand, but in that moment I felt abandoned, like I was only worth friendship if I was still with Betty, no matter if they did or didn't hear my side of the story. It was then that I remembered back to a time we were all drinking together as couples and I spilled out that I didn't trust Hillary because she wasn't reliable. That memory coupled with this cold shoulder on a cold night in an unknown town was all I ever needed to know about her again. I called Suze, who had saved my skin when I came through Berkeley the first time and asked her if I could stay with her again and she agreed. Suze, a relative stranger 1, Hillary 0.

I made my way to Suze and she greeted me as an old friend. I bestowed on her a handful of weed from the farm and she thanked me. I told her I felt I was ready to try LSD and was going to look for some once I got back to LA. It was strange that I wrote for a psychedelic webzine, but hadn't tried the all-time classic LSD. She perked up and handed me some foil. "Inside here is the best acid I've had in a really long time. Take it!" I received it with thanks and told her my plans to see my good pals, Albert and Macy in Pasadena. We stayed up and talked for a while, but I was worn from the road and was going to try to make LA by the next night, so I turned in. The next morning when I awoke, Suze had already gone to work and I left a thank you note and hit the road.

I had hoped I could see Peacock since she lived in the same general area, but she was out of town at the time, so I carried on back down the road through the hills that lie between San Francisco and the mighty I-5. Dappled along the way were armies of wind turbines that swirled and swung like they were running in place. Every time I saw them they filled me with hope, as if they were promises of a future not so bleak, like we could do something good with the resources so readily available to us. As I blasted down the road, Dylan set the tone. On and on I went till I hit that speedway beset on both sides by orange groves as far as the eye could see. The groves gave way to crops and then desert, with tumbleweeds stuck in the fences along the highway. As I pulled in for gas my phone rang. It was my son Gideon calling to say hi out of the blue. I told him I was coming for Christmas and we discussed our visit. He hung up and I felt amazing. Almost back! Almost home! As I gassed up I noticed my back tire was shredded from all that wildness in the hills trying to escape. There were deep gouges in the tires, but not so deep that they would cause any real problems. I just looked at the long strips of missing tire and laughed to myself at the ridiculousness of what I had just been through.

*Clear golden light
from the source.
Good fortune.*

I CHING, HEXAGRAM 30, LINE 2

Chapter 14

THE SUN BEGAN TO SET AS I DESCENDED from the hills into the great expanse of the Los Angeles area. That flat, overpopulated, piece-of-shit city never looked so good. I made my way to Pasadena, where my friends Albert and Macy awaited my arrival. When I got there, I received a king's welcome. I walked in and greeted their kitten who had grown much bigger than last time I saw him, gave Macy a hug, and handed Albert a hash ball the size of a large marble. His eyes turned big and he smiled like a Cheshire cat as he hurriedly grabbed his smoking equipment. I told him about the strain of weed I had been working with, how it was soothing and soft rather than the normal buzzing and frenetic high that so many other strains delivered. He took a hit and smiled in agreement. I had the good shit. We spent the remainder of the evening drinking wine and smoking my fine variety of ganja and I shared my tales from the road. When I mentioned that I had some LSD, they both agreed that we all should do it together. So we decided to go to a Huntington Gardens in Pasadena where we could roam and explore and feel confident that we might do this without too much trouble from others.

The next day came and we were all filled with the nervous excitement that comes before almost any psychedelic event. I might have been the most nervous since I had never done LSD before and was concerned about the length of time that it lasted. Sure, I had been on many trips that are reportedly much more intense than acid, but one must never approach an experience like this with terse erudition unless one is willing to get a psychic reprimand from the forces that seem to work within the psychedelic realm.

We left the house around eleven AM and got bagels from a local shop. After we had eaten, we each took two hits of the acid and I saved two more for later. I had assumed that it would take a while to kick in, as mushrooms normally do, but I almost instantly felt different. As we drove, we reassured each other we would be kind above all things and never fuck with each other while we were high. We said our "I love yous" and found parking outside of the park. It was by this time that I began to feel strange and euphoric. Sounds began to take on a different life, color began to twist and brighten. The very first clear indication of a change in awareness came as I followed Macy along the path that led us into the park. She stepped in a puddle that had formed from the sprinklers watering the

Clear Golden Light

grass and as it splashed it became the only thing I noticed, but it was strange and wonderful. Instead of just a splash, it was the primordial birth, an echo of a bigger bang, the cry of a baby ocean, and the song of water.

A soft, but tenuous suspicion arose over me as we passed a lurching, aged security guard whose sickly coiffed grey hair and oversized clothing lent to the idea that he was both mischievous and villainously looking for those who might try to Scooby Doo their way into his park for acid fueled hijinx. We had all been in enough situations collectively to approach this kind of suspicion with grace and psychonautical confidence, leaving this towering lackluster man in blue unaware of our inner workings. When we made our way to the admissions gate we were beset on all sides by white and purple haired elderly rich women, affluent Asian mothers, and overly tanned out of shape Pasadenians. The park was essentially a zoo without any animals, expansive and confusing, but also full of intrigue.

There is little mystery in how I looked, following Albert and Macy like a puppy with a cartoonish grin that I had already begun to battle as we slinked into the vast park. As if running in an obstacle course, we were confronted by yet another daunting task, which was to accept a park map from a chatty man just past the entrance. He began to speak with Albert about where to go and what to do and so on, but what really interested me was the fact that I could hear the five conversations going on with anyone in earshot and could articulate the goings on of all of them. It was as if I had become momentarily omnipresent and capable of superhuman perception. This to me was far more interesting than the burdensome conversation of locations of things that Albert was forced to engage in with the chatty fellow. As we finally broke free I giggled to myself and told Albert and Macy about what I had been experiencing. "Oh yeah, it's pretty wild!" Albert replied as if it were as common to him as peeling a banana, or making coffee. Macy, like myself was a newcomer to LSD and so we took a certain amount of kinship in that notion of exploring the unknown together.

We made our way through a path along a wooded area, but in the periphery I could hear the whooshing of exercise pants behind me. I tried to ignore it, but had to look and saw a small Asian woman with a sun visor and oversized glasses making her way along a parallel path. Again, I could not help but think that perhaps she was some sort of alien observer who was monitoring our progress as we Forest Gump'd our way through the pathway. For one reason or another, there was an inordinate amount of Asian people there that day. I say this with no malice, but there is a certain way that some behave that has a sort of sneakiness about it. A run is never a run, but more of a walk that is not totally committed to running. A walk is never just a walk, but a meticulously observed scissor-

Clear Golden Light

like execution of leg movement that takes one purposefully from one objective to the next. The camera-clad curiosity with which many of those there carried themselves filled me with a dread of discovery, like I would be found out and properly documented with all of those cameras. I did my best not to make broad-stroked characterizations like this, but I could not help but notice this tendency as I goofily capered behind Albert and Macy.

We settled in a big open field and enjoyed the sunshine and people watching. We saw a feature in the grass where a spiral had been formed with raised grassy knolls and fancied that we might lay in the ruts, but to our disappointment the ruts were a point of attraction for thousands of gnats which swarmed overhead. Considering our mental state, these gnats took on a special significance; their dancing and swarming had rhythm and a method, which made them more like dancing molecules than tiny creatures. The heightened edge detection that psychedelics provided made this beyond High Definition to almost a transdimensional degree. Even so, they were disgusting and might make us prone to some hallucinatory freak out that none of us were interested in trying out, so we opted for a bench at the edge of the field where we could be ridiculous with little interruption or suspicion of tripping.

We sat and lay there on a blanket watching the grass and looking at one another as if we had never seen a human so beautiful. Albert's black full beard grew from his face like the regal roots of an ancient tree, while his oversized smile reassured of safety. Between the three of us, there was this sense of absolute love and solidarity; almost like a force field that protected us from the rank and obscenely jejune world that bombarded us daily with its sullen tones and fragrant permeation of bullshit. As I looked at Macy, her eyes seemed to glow with a holy light that filled the open air with an azure radiance that aped the magnificence of a clear Mediterranean sea. She was and is always beautiful, but in that time and space, I understood what holy feminine radiance was, so far beyond sexuality and brute attraction that it filled me with a sense of divine awe. This again mirrored the radiance that Albert in all of his manly prowess and grace had exuded in that time and space.

We lay there observing the surroundings and the nonsensical seriousness with which we approach the everyday world. Our daily life gone on unnoticed and unobserved became a laughable festival of idiocy, blind consumerism and hollow faith, while we little laughing Buddhas took a judgment-free respite from these hang ups and enjoyed the nonsense for what it really was. For that couple of hours, we became detached from the intoxicating delusion of what we were normally convinced was "real".

Off in the distance, I observed a woman pushing a baby in its carriage. She stopped and ornately laid out the blanket onto the perfect grass and

Clear Golden Light

pulled the baby from its holster. I couldn't help but be fascinated, as she appeared to fold the helpless creature into the grass, as if the grass itself could be wrapped around to swaddle the little fat-faced human larvæ. It was then that I mused out loud how the baby felt at that moment, being helplessly plunged from the comfort of the rolling anti-coffin and left to flail vigorously in the open field while mother ruthlessly took photos of it. I could only imagine how she felt and what she was thinking, "Oh I am going to send these photos to everyone and they will love the baby and will love me! They will congratulate me for having received sperm and nine months later producing this new creature!" I tried to whisper these thoughts as they came and narrated these ideas to Albert and Macy who both were unsuccessfully trying to withhold giggles and short outbursts of horror that we might be overheard and found out as balls trippers. On the periphery, the visored whooshing lady walked by again.

Without warning Macy blurted out, "Eww, this grass looks really dead!" Albert and I looked at the grass and looked at each other, seeing the lush surroundings and considered that maybe Macy had a stronger dose than us. Albert gently reassured her that it was beautiful and that maybe we should take a look around. At this point, standing up, looking at people, speaking, holding hands, not holding hands, or virtually any action we could perform might be suspect. I can only be utterly thankful that Albert and Macy would so graciously come with me, this giant goofball that I had further become under the influence of Hofmann's mystic elixir. It seemed that nothing I could do or say would be perceived as normal, but I did my best to hold it together. This was easier said than done.

As we explored the grounds we came across a pond with lilypads, water-bound flowers, and an abundance of koi fish. These fish were quite large, the biggest ones reaching about a foot and a half in size. As we approached the pond the koi came to the edge and extended their heads out of the water, no doubt hoping that we had food to throw at them, but what I saw was absolutely shocking. These fish seemed to cry out to me as if they were humans trapped in the bodies of fish. Their flesh took on a human tone as the heavenly whites and too orange for oranges swirled over their bodies as they shimmered and writhed at the water's edge. Their mouths extended out like a mute fool's hand begging for money, for food, for mercy. It was then that I felt that I myself was no different from those fish as they wriggled desperately for something that they did not even know of, or understand, they only knew that they wanted it and it seemed ever out of their reach. I was the reach of their mouths, their destitution of meaning, the limbless, rubber reactionary spasms, mindless and hungry, fumbling in the void, grasping for the ineffable. This was that mad feeling I had so strongly felt when I first left

Clear Golden Light

LA, now dancing before me as a swarm of desperate fish. I revealed my insight into these humanoid fish to Albert and Macy, but my description was too much for Macy, and she begged us to move on.

Chapter 15

WE CAME TO A SMALL BAMBOO FOREST FULL of dense, tall shoots in the deepest of greens. Walking along the path in the bamboo forest felt wonderful, mystical, and soothing as the color and cool air of the shade calmed us. As I came around a corner in the path I looked and saw a giant statue of a baby and exclaimed without warming, "You guys, there's a giant fucking baby at the water's edge!" Macy laughed and gave an Oh my God as she and Albert turned the corner to investigate my claim. Just as I had said, there was a giant statue of a baby at the water's edge. We all burst into laughter at the ridiculousness of somebody being commissioned thousands of dollars to make that baby statue and feature it here in this people zoo that we found ourselves in. We laughed hysterically for a moment before trying to calm ourselves enough to make it to the bathroom.

The bathrooms were across a clearing and we felt a bit like deer in the wild, unsure of the presence of predators, but we all gave each other a pep talk and began to make our way across the field. There were two bathrooms and so Albert and Macy went first, leaving me to my own devices in the field. As I sat there, the visor-clad Asian woman whooshed across a nearby path, and I dared not look right at her lest she stop and stare voiceless at me. I sat there giggling to myself trying to not look suspect, but it was futile. I was wearing a black sweater in seventy degree heat and was sweating profusely, red faced and gleeful. After what seemed a torturous eternity Albert and Macy reemerged from their respective potty dens and reported their findings. "The blow dryer is terrifying in there! Just wipe your hands on your clothes after you wash them!" Macy exclaimed. Just then, as I approached, a female groundskeeper pulled up on a four-wheeler and tended to one of the bathrooms. It now left me with the foreboding realization that whatever I did in that bathroom would be closely monitored and heard by this would-be assassin.

I walked in as cool a manner as I could muster, being oafish and sweaty, opening and closing the door in a mechanical fashion. I made my way to the urinal and went pee, trying not to look at anything in particular since having my genitals exposed in this condition added to my sense of vulnerability. I didn't flush, fearing the roar, but washed my hands and walked out with a secretive and hurried walk. Albert and Macy stood there smiling and giggling. I was highly giggly as well and was having trouble taking in everything that

Clear Golden Light

I was receiving without commentary, or overt expression of wonder.

Albert led us around the corner to the southwestern garden that featured innumerable cacti of all varieties. It was as if we had been thrust into an alien landscape. There were many people there, which especially put Macy on high alert. She doted upon my every action, warning me not to touch the cacti, but I couldn't help it. These living creatures that stood still were like squid that lived on land. These pokey and spindled beings were cephalopods that you could touch and observe for long periods of time. My nonsense was becoming too much though, and the place was just too exquisite for me to handle without outbursts of wonder and amazement.

As we made our way out of the cactus garden, a water fountain beckoned me, but it was close to several groups of Asians taking pictures of cacti and sage and talking boisterously. As I approached the water fountain, I had that all-too-common stoner thought of "I have to look like I'm not high and it's funny that I'm high and maybe people don't know it but I've got to play it cool, but fuck, I'm going to burst into laughter, oh god don't burst into laughter keep it cool, man!" Albert and Macy had gone on autopilot and were making their way back to the field without noticing that I was stuck trying to sneak my way to the fountain unnoticed by the throng of Asian camera people. I took one drink and then two and then tried to fill my mouth with water so I could escape like a hungry seagull from the potential dangers that surrounded me, but the thought was too humorous to me and I spat out the water and burst into tearful laughter in front of the throng, who looked at me in that perplexed and astonished way that only a group of camera-clad Asians might. I ran like a child who had shit himself to Albert and Macy, who both covered their faces in laugh-filled horror at the spectacle I had just created. It was after this that it became painfully clear that we needed to return to the safety of our home base at the edge of the large field in which we had settled previously if we were to remain in the park without further incident.

We had made it back unscathed from the water fountain debacle and just looked around. I laid myself down on the blanket on the grass and closed my eyes in silence. It was then that a moment I had been desperately waiting for finally came. With my eyes closed and the sun beating through my eyelids, the red glow of sunlight fell like love upon me and filled me from head to toe with spectral warmth that perhaps only the womb had given me before. A plural telepathic voice, quiet and feminine spoke to me.

"Gabriel, we brought you here so that you would get here. We told you to come to the wilderness and gave you this hunger so that you would come. If we had not given you the call and the hunger, you would not have ever gotten where you

want to be, where you are destined to be. Do you understand? Did you think that this quest would end after forty days with a dimensional portal opening and you escaping this plane of existence? You did, we know. We know that you desire the other, you desire us, but we are not as you are and you are not ready for us, but you are going as we have called you and we will be with you and have never been far from you since the day you were born. This is only the beginning, not an end".

I understood. I knew that the visions I had last year that called me to spend forty days in the wilderness were real, that this kind of prophetic calling was real. For here I was on the other side of forty days in the wilds of Northern California a new man, a different one. That is, not to say perfected, but better, stronger, and keener to the voice of that divine wisdom that lives in the place between sleep and waking, coitus and death, meditation and psychedelic vision. That collective spoke to me as one voice, as the Gnostic Sophia, as Green Tara, one and the same. And there lying in this living euphoria, this Pauline vision of the divine, the blood vessels and flesh made an impossible hybrid vision of stained glass made of my own flesh and blood. It was what theologians traditionally refer to as a theophany, but in feminine guise. I had received another kind of sight, one that had nothing to do with physical vision, but that of the visionary.

The grass rose and fell like the earth was breathing in and out. The softness beneath me was like an earthen bed, supple and natural. As we observed the trees they waved at us like a thousand women doing Tai Chi in unison, and all of creation sang the song of wind and the danced the dance of trees, flowers, and birds. We were breathlessly in awe as we clamored and explored under that clear deep blue sky. As we made our way to the exit we passed a bridge and a waterfall. It astounded me with beauty and I called to Albert and Macy to stop with me there. "Do you hear it guys? The waterfall is speaking with legion tongues with a message from space". We all stood transfixed at the audio-visual miracle that endlessly unfolded before us as if it were the answer to everything.

We walked across another field and I looked to Albert and Macy walking in the honey golden sun, the scientist and his starlet, arms across each other's shoulders as they walked. The miracle of love and beauty that exploded from them was so strong it blinded my loneliness. Its ample brilliance blotted out my sins of love and gave me a glimpse of what is, could be, and might be again. In a way, that moment might have been all I really needed to see in this life to have hope.

We successfully made it out of the park and a wave of relief and accomplishment swept over us, only to be followed by a new concern, especially on Macy's behalf. "Albert, are you okay to drive like this?" Albert replied with a Dawkinsian level

Clear Golden Light

of certitude, "Babe, I've done this a million times. I could drive on acid with my eyes closed!" I could tell this didn't reassure her, but she literally went along for the ride. We were nearing the Los Angeles rush hour and the roads were jam-packed with a diaspora of attractions from the invading and mundane world around us. The joke was everywhere, on the faces of the frustrated drivers, the oversized ads for the local gym, the fat fellow in the pink cowboy hat riding along the crosswalk on a BMX; it was all ridiculous and all too normal for everyone but us. Albert drove naturally and we were put to relative ease, till all of the sudden a woman backed her car out of her driveway without looking and at full speed. Albert slammed on his brakes and yelled out, "No, don't mind me! I'm just tripping on ACID!" After the initial shock of almost being in a wreck, we carried on home and settled down in front of their fireplace.

The LSD came in waves. We thought we were out of the woods, but then it would come back. On those lulls there was this sensation like metal wire was running through my veins and it was as uncomfortable as it sounds. This led Macy to go from waves of quiet pain to joyful exuberance. Being home livened her up and allowed her to express herself without the worry of prying eyes. It was during one of these high tides that she insisted that we all do DMT. I knew that they had some and that they had done it many times before, but it is not a trifle; it is in fact the most astonishing thing I think can be done. The tone of the room grew grim as Albert and I had the sobering realization that we might have to take that big leap, the blast into lightspeed and machine elf mystery. The look on Albert's face is something I'll never forget, his eyes big as saucers gazed at the floor as if he had just gotten death-sentence test results.

Macy in an uncharacteristic fit of boldness asked me again if I really wanted to pass up going through it. I couldn't say no, I wanted to go for it, but I tried my best not to think about it until the time actually came. I went to the bathroom and watched the walls breathe in and out as I had a pee. I washed my hands on the swollen towel that took on the likeness of the carcass of a cookie monster slain and walked to the couch where Macy and Albert had prepared the wax bong. They lit it and put the DMT in, I breathed in as long and deep as I could and held it.

As the LSD and DMT met, they dissolved my body into a hundred-thousand electric bees and with the Snap, Crackle and Pop I was thrust into a giant domed structure the size of a sports stadium. And there in that vast expanse where I was alone the walls and ceiling shimmered with diamonds, rubies, bone, ivory, emeralds, sapphires and every other precious thing in blinding shades of white. Then she arrived in the corner of my mind's eye, *her, she,* the Divine Feminine. I yelled out in the physical, "It's her! It's her!" She was the one from my first big trip in my Queens apartment, she was

Clear Golden Light

the serpent in the center of the earth who called me to the desert; it was HER!

She said to me as she tread across the roof of the dome, "Of course it's me, dummy! I'm she who dances to keep the world full of splendor". Without her dancing, all beauty in the universe would disappear and be lost forever. I was not allowed to see her, only the imprint of her foot as it tread, like the wind leaves its imprint on dunes. As she tread across the dome, the roof rained fine jewels like floating feathers, pearls dripping like milk. She had spoken to me earlier in that day, but it was like I was in the Holy of Holies, and she had me as a captive audience in a reality that is more real than any I had ever known. The vision waned and I returned to my LSD state, which was beginning to fade and told Albert and Macy about my experience.

I went to bed glowing from the majestic experience, but feeling the bitter bite of the comedown, which in honesty felt very painful and chemical. The next day I told David Metcalfe and Dr. August about my experiences and was shocked to hear that my experience with the Divine Feminine was a dead ringer for visions of Tara:

O Tara white as the autumn moon,
Milk of a hundred lunations
Treasure of Clarity, flowing with Wisdom.
Light of a thousand galaxies.

*Goddess All-Knowing, Red Kurukulla
Your mantras fill the three realms;
Seven worlds crumble beneath your feet,
Your magic attracts every being.*

*O Goddess Fortuna, dripping with jewels,
Crowned by the bright crescent moon
The primordial Buddha of infinite light
blazes from your high-gathered locks.*

*O Mahashanti, luminous bliss,
From the fields of absolute peace,
By the mantra Svaha and the primordial Om
You dissolve the deepest of fears.*

Dr. August informed me that visions of Tara involve jewels dripping from her feet. I was absolutely floored that I hadn't just had some random hallucination, but had quite literally had an encounter with the divine feminine, the resplendent rainbow serpent, the Gnostic Sophia, it was her!

Chapter 16

I RETRIEVED MANY OF MY BELONGINGS THAT I had not seen for two months and it felt a bit like an early Christmas present. It was early December after all. After enjoying the company of Albert and Macy in the warmth and solace of their home Albert took me to the bus stop in downtown LA where I hopped a Greyhound bus back up to my home state of Washington. I said my goodbye to Albert and got on the bus. My parents had offered for me to stay with them as they had plenty of room, so I opted to set up shop there for December. The ride to Seattle was twenty-six hours long. I tried to sleep, but the seating was uncomfortable and the bus seemed to stop every half hour or so at some new locale. I did my best to rest, to read, and to write, but mostly it was a new kind of meditation in which I decided to sit with the pain of immobility.

I was greeted with hugs and joyful commiseration at my parents' house where we broke open some wine and played pool straightaway. I was welcome and warm and had no need of anything, at least in that moment.

When I made mention of my return to Washington on social media, my old friend, Svetlana offered to hang out. Now I had never had any romantic dealings with Svetlana, but she was certainly a sight for sore eyes, especially for a man who had been thrown to the breeze for a couple of months. We met up in Seattle. I had forgotten how boisterous and lively she was and reveled in the joy of her bubbly, yet well-read mannerisms. We went for coffee and she told me about how shitty Seattle was. "Everyone here is doing the same thing they were doing when you left here six years ago. All the dudes are pussies, or are drunk all the time, or have moved on from cocaine to meth and all the girls have slept with all the guys who still might be good. It sucks and I'm tired of dealing with these crappy people!" Her remarks reminded me of my life in NYC.

"In New York, there is a culling of talent because people in the smaller towns are dissatisfied with the quality of people and opportunity in their own, so they move to New York. What happens then is that there is a huge amount of good-looking, smart, well-educated, and world-class talented individuals that people New York. It's hard to go from that to anywhere else because of this and it's the reason why I miss it so much". But looking across at Svetlana, I didn't mind being in Seattle for a bit. We moved on to a Vietnamese

Clear Golden Light

soup place down the street in the Fremont district and discussed what we might do for the night. I had completely run out of money since my time in the NorCal hills and was hoping to go to a house party, or visit a mutual friend. We had planned to visit with our friend Yvette, who was a notorious party animal: part time rock and roll slut and all around good time. Yvette however was feeling under the weather, leaving Svetlana and I to our own devices.

We walked along the waterway and talked until the walkway stopped, carrying on and catching up on each other's wins and losses. She was hard to read, not distant, but not giving any indications if she was open to there being something between us or not. Given my still relative freshly broken up status, I was in no position to start a new relationship, but I also had been alone and left on my own for what felt like a long time. We stopped in at Hattie's Hat in Ballard and had two vodkas each. As we walked out, it became more readily apparent that she might be interested in something romantic unfolding, so I grabbed her by her hips and pulled the back of her head firmly and placed my lips to hers. In an instant she opened like a time-lapsed rose at the kiss of daylight and let out a sound of pleasured relief.

We made our way back to my truck. The thing sat by the seaside at my father's house and smelled like an old boat. Svetlana said it was an endearing scent to her. Neither of us were strangers to cobbled together cars, people, or situations. In fact we were both used to and fond of those types of things. I gave her a big handful of my amazing weed and let her smoke some. She asked if I wanted to go on an adventure and I agreed, so she guided me as I drove to a graveyard at the top of Queen Anne hill and we crept quietly in. I followed her to a stone just after we each took a drag of the good stuff. "This is where my grandparents are". And as quickly as she said it she pulled to me and kissed me. Svetlana was thin, but well curved with contours like a Corvette. Her hand crept down to a place where no woman's hand had gone for quite some time and I came to life. And there we were in the dark of the graveyard, agents of Eros and Thanatos embodying sex and death. This magical concept was not lost on me and fueled further excitement.

She was staying with some friends and was bound to sleep on a couch that night. I would be forced to ride the ferry back to the peninsula at my paternal home. While driving I couldn't help but imagine her laid out on a bed postured and prone with her stiletto legs crossing and sliding across one another in anticipation. As I pulled up to the house, Svetlana thanked me for the night and reached over to kiss me. But the kiss did not undo itself, instead it livened and turned to fire. She crawled onto me in the driver's seat and brought me to life once more and kissed me and brought my head to her breast. It became clear to me that this situation would not do, so I offered to get us a

Clear Golden Light

hotel. She nodded yes in flustered excitement.

It took us an hour to find a place suitable and we grabbed some essentials from the corner store nearby. When we got to the room she unfolded before me with her celestial body and we clung to each other, if only for that time and place, like death was at our doorstep and this was our last night. Afterwards, I drew bathwater for her and sat naked beside the tub. Her petite body was covered in water and suds and I could not resist but to climb inside the tub with her. I put on Leonard Cohen and we held each other in the water, as hot as we could stand it and listened to the song that loomed overhead. The soft and warm tones of the lyrics lulled like an opiate and we both sunk into steamed hypnosis, breathing in the white mist and watching the drops of water collect and fall down bare flesh.

We stayed there in that heat and steam and just let ourselves go, soft and gentle, allowing our recoiled love lines to reach out to one another. We were both respectively broken for reasons we didn't need to explain. We knew each other long enough to not have to say those things. We just were, there and then, and it was lovely. As the night lingered on we lay in bed draped upon one another, soaking in that prolonged moment, dreading the coming of daylight, which would drive us like vampires back to our quietude, loneliness, and respective winter wandering. I took Svetlana home and thanked her for a wonderful night and we agreed to be in touch. A few days later I spoke with my friend Goldie, who had an interest in getting a drink with me and we agreed to do so the next week. I met up with her at a bar on Capitol Hill, just a couple blocks from her apartment. She was thin and fashionably dressed with stern features perfect for a high-powered businesswoman in New York, but she was firmly fixed in Seattle. Her eyes were bright and her alluring smile indicated high intelligence. The bartender fixed me up an Old-Fashioned with mescal rather than bourbon. We sat and caught up. Goldie wrote for a local paper and some web publications, had traveled extensively, and was properly educated at a solid university. Her vocabulary and reference to great literature punctuated her sentences in a fashion that did not overwhelm, but showed a level of sophistication rarely found in the Capitol Hill types. The area was my old stomping ground. I had spent eight years prior doing nefarious things and gangster activities, making sure the hipsters of the Hill had their party favors. I once famously put a man through the window at the Cha Cha after inciting a fight there. Those days were over and I was a very different person now, minimally-internet famous and established as an author and authority on fringe theology and psychedelic fieldwork.

Goldie and I easily kept pace with each other in our conversations, especially in the intersection between eastern and western ideals. I was drawn to her listless styling as a writer and her piquant

Clear Golden Light

use of rare English words without succumbing to the dangers of pretense. She embodied longing so much that the word was literally tattooed on her body. It was in many ways a firm connection that seemed fortuitous. As the drinks continued, I told her that I could not have more since I needed to travel for two hours to the peninsula. She offered for me to stay at her place instead. I went and re-parked my truck where it would be safe for the night and came back in. It was then that the tone took a turn toward that playful sort of drunken testing of waters people do when they both want to fuck, but are trying to get a clearer green light.

It was strange being back in Seattle after all these years and in many ways it felt like nothing had changed. The only thing that did change was the crowd that swarmed Capitol Hill. Where once it had really just been hipsters and gays, it was now dominated by condos and girls dressed like they were out on prom night. The cocktails went from simple standards like Pabst and well whiskey to the mescal Old-Fashioned in my hand. Things were the same, but different. Back in the day, I had my run of the place and now I was in my mid-thirties, broken, and back in town. I wasn't sure whether I should be embarrassed, excited, or some other third thing. But I was there across from Goldie, pretty, whip-smart, and increasingly sexual in overtones as the cocktails went down.

She and I kept pace and we tumbled down the street to her place. We got in and she went into the bathroom. I slipped into pajamas like a good domesticated man and was planning to offer that we head straight to sleep. By this time though, Goldie had other plans. She came into the room like an angry wrestler and straddled me, kissing me forcefully. This unexpected move turned me off and I offered not to sleep with her then and there. She asked me why and I responded that my heart was broken and that I was unfit for female consumption. She said she understood and acknowledged that she wouldn't be trying to make me her own. I felt a certain softness return to her as opposed to the aggression that seemed to overtake her moments before.

I felt as though I was speaking and acting as women in my past had, using lines they had used as a deterrent for sex. What the fuck was going on with me? I slept beside her, my body contouring hers. There in the muted cobalt of the city light creeping through the cracks, I could see the silhouette of her beautiful body and hear the soft sound of her breath as she slept. I ran my hand down her thigh softly and slowly and she whimpered of wakefulness. I ran my hand the other direction up toward her breast and she again breathed out a relieved sigh as she ran her leg against mine. Without a word she placed her hand on me and guided me in as we slowly moved in unison in the dark. Her breath smelled of tequila but her swaying and shifting kept me occupied, and we moved with more verve and vigor until we both reached a fever

Clear Golden Light

pitch of sweat and rapture. When morning came, she was up early and getting ready to go to work. Once again and without a word she came and got on me once more before hurrying out the door. "Don't fuck up my house! Eat what you want, it's all girly bird food, but go for it. I'll see you soon!" I got up and made myself two eggs and tidied up everything. Headed back out to the peninsula to go Christmas shopping for my kids. I messaged Goldie with thanks and offered to come see her again soon.

Chapter 17

CHRISTMAS WAS A SOMBER EVENT, OFFERING a lonesome outpost of the family homestead out on the peninsula as safe harbor, but what of friends, lovers, and compatriots? This Christmas was a far cry from the nights of gaiety that flooded my Brooklyn apartment with Betty as we gathered all of our friends, New York miscreants who were all orphans from other places. We exchanged cocktails and did blow off each other, smacking asses and raising a holy ruckus. In Bushwick, Christmas sounded very similar to any given day, or night; loud as fuck and full of raw, visceral revelry. Back here on what felt like a remote outpost, the somber water glistened and my heart swelled like a frozen water balloon. It was then that I pined for Betty in all of her imperfection, selfishness, blindness, and buxom somatic overflow. We exchanged a couple messages back and forth. I didn't want her back, but she still represented a comfort to me, a home that was no more.

The day after Christmas, I picked up my kids and we enjoyed our time together out at the cabin on the peninsula with my dad and stepmother. The kids were overjoyed that I was in the area again and confessed that they loved New York and LA, but just wanted me more. I had to look back at all that time I was trying to prove something to some unknown person, a golem made up of everyone who ever doubted me, and find a way to crush it. In the old and dirty days when I ran with Tahoe and Hank, twin brothers who raised hell, I moved cocaine for a guy named Big Man, dated a slender, ginger nineteen-year-old, and did gangster shit. Nobody trusted me after all that. I "used to be so good", they thought; rumors swirled about my activity. These were the workings of the golem that bore the face of my Antichrist step-brother, my frowning, high-voiced sister, and raised-chinned mother. This monster might as well have bought my ticket to New York and moved my shit into my apartment. This monster got me on the bus to work fourteen- and sixteen-hour days at that New Jersey airport where the private jets fly. This monster made me marry to show how successful I was, and this monster, this golem in my mind that was made up of all of these people and ideas, robbed me of my children. This monster was me. I fought this fucking thought-golem for seven or eight years only to find myself once again washed upon the shores of the Puget Sound like some shipwrecked drunk: divorced, jobless, a "writer"

Clear Golden Light

and grad school hopeful. Nobody but my brother, my dad and step-mom, and my kids gave two shits about me. Well, they gave a shit and that's all I needed. They and Svetlana and Goldie, that is. The few were good though, and sometimes the kind of care and how much are not nearly as important as just *some* kind of care.

My kids seemed to understand what was going on with me more than anyone else did. Maybe I trained them well to know the oddball "wisdom" of my ways. They both had grown so fast and I knew I had made the right decision to come up to Washington for the holidays. My dad had suggested over and over that I consider moving back to Washington permanently, but I was set on going to a small university in LA for their grad program in philosophy. Besides, I had a book tour I was hoping to assemble with money from the sale of the Gnostic Rocket once I got back to California. That was the plan and I was going to see it through, finance my first year of school, and make a fresh start.

I had two choices around that cold holiday season as it lurched into a new year: stay in the safe but remote confines of the familial grounds, or venture into the spindled arms of Goldie, whose breathless tones in rapture danced like honey-tipped feathers in an updraft. She was fraught with paradox; bold and empowered, yet needy and jealous as a child. More than anything it was nice to be around somebody who wrote so well; somebody who could tell me things that impressed me. Perhaps it's the sign of the times, or perhaps it has always been, but people say dumb shit constantly; the kind of conversations held by people who fill their sentences with the next sequence of meaningless events. "Oh, are you going to Kara's after Havanna? Yeah, I think we're going to go. Did you get a hold of your dealer? God I love that new 'TV on the radio' song!" If I could defecate in public, the privilege might be utilized at a moment of content like that. I might even throw it, like a spider monkey. These kinds of thoughts are exactly what Goldie would enjoy sharing with me and we shared camaraderie in our lofty disgust.

"I can't be your boyfriend, I can be all yours when I am with you, but I am damaged goods going through a divorce" I said to Goldie. "Yeah, that's cool, I get it" she said, embodying her best "dude" impression as she thinly nodded in downward-faced agreement. But this was not to be the case, because with every night I slept in her bed and every time she took me inside, she would say "I love you". And when she was drunk she would shake me and pull at my manhood and tell me like it was an emergency. I knew this was no good, but was it her, or was it my good sense telling me that this would not end well?

We spent Super Bowl Sunday at the Cha Cha, a local haunt that I had frequented during my drug pushing years. There on the big screen we watched as the Seahawks turned the Broncos into keystone cops before the eyes of every blue-blooded American. Neither of us had money, but Goldie had a

Clear Golden Light

million ex-boyfriends and one of them saw her and bought us both drinks. As I sat there watching the mad display, I couldn't help but sear over the insidious ruse that was our life. Only a couple months prior, I was among the rabble of the highway, the gutter punks and bums, burners and college students avoiding the long dick of the law as we all tried to squeeze money out of the marijuana industry while the gettin' was still good. I looked around at the frat boys and silk-shirted jerkoffs who had money to burn and wondered to myself what we were doing. Across the world we were still in that endless ploy called war, as useless to freedom as the war on drugs is to sobriety. It was not even considered.

While our favorite brown men stood in billion-dollar football fields, our brown savage enemies bled into dusty, foreign killing fields. One brown man praised God for a touchdown and one praised God for another dead American, but only the ball game was televised. This was the vision of our forefathers, who no doubt nodded in pioneering pride to know that Walmarts would be fully stocked with starving workers on food stamps and the lowest prices we could negotiate from the Chinese slave factories. The giant, Seattle-based aviation companies of the world could pay Military-Industrial-Complex-fueled paychecks to all of us North Westerners so we could buy them cheap trinkets, season tickets, and Legion of Boom swag. In a way, the weapons of war paid for the game. Oh yeah, we just got another touchdown.

I couldn't help but feel sad for all of us, like the pity you have for a rich kid whose trust fund had run out. It just felt like we were doing something evil and this evil was one of the few things that brought us Americans together. Goldie and I made our way back to Pony, a local gay bar owned by my old pal Ursula. We dropped in and said hi to her friend, Vicki. Vicki was a ball of energy and humor with a smile like the Eskimo on the side of Alaska Airlines tail fins. Vicki took a shine to me immediately and we became insta-buddies. We had a couple of drinks and made our way back to Goldie's place and painted each other with magic symbols and hit the sheets.

Chapter 18

IT WAS AT THIS TIME THAT I PUT THE FINAL touches on my third book and polished it up for publishing. I still had an interview with Danielle Bolelli, a fascinating college professor who made a name for himself as a kind of Daoist Badboy. He wrote a book about building a custom religion like Bruce Lee built his form of Kung Fu. When I interviewed him, he struck a chord that changed the nature of what I was looking for on this big change I was going through. Afterall, I was doing all of this to find that next level of Hermetic knowledge. I wasn't sure what the message was, or where it could be found. I talked to him over the phone.

"There is this ascetic path followed by obscure wandering mystics who are living off what they can find; I've actually been living that way for the last three months and it's been really weird and wild and it hasn't been easy but I've always found some sort of fortuitous occasion or connection. A couple nights ago, a guy got me a beer because he said he had a dream that he saw me and he wasn't hitting on me, he was like "I had a dream and I saw you", and I said let me read your tarot and I read tarot and he said 'Oh this is amazing, let me buy you a beer!', and I was like 'Okay!' and I didn't have any money but I mean this is kind of how those guys operate and it's crazy, it's crazy to our civilization. But I mean, is there magic? Do people do this? And likewise, why don't we all just go to a mountain to become enlightened, I suppose because there's not enough mountains?"

"Right?" Danielle responded, "there's something to be said about searching for enlightenment in the midst of the everyday world. In the midst of the struggles and the complications of it all, the lonely hermit on the mountain, I don't want to say it's too easy but it's an enlightenment that's born outside of being tested by the everyday forces that mess people up; it's one that is better than no enlightenment at all and is in my mind actually inferior to being able to deal with all the seven million contradictions that life entails".

"That's such a poignant thought", I replied, fascinated, "and this actually happened to me when I was describing what was going on to a traveling companion that I had; they were like 'Well what do you think is harder? To be out in the desert by yourself, living beans and rice, sitting by a fire meditating, or to have to do the exact same thing but you're in a city and there's no public toilets and you have to have money to have transporation

Clear Golden Light

anywhere. What's the more difficult task?'"

"And also one is more applicable to many other contexts", Danielle added, "whereas the other is sort of stacking when you are outside of most regular human interaction, you're outside of jobs, you're outside most of the same thing which most other humans live in. So then the question is either you live that way your whole life, or you return to the reality that most people inhabit; but then how you deal with it? Is that enlightenment learned in the desert something that can last if brought back in, or does it only work in its own space?"

I thought for days about what Danielle had said. *Is that enlightenment learned in the desert something that can last if brought back in, or does it only work in its own space?* This was precisely my question, because I had been on the mountain, and now I had come back. And while I was a man transformed and illuminated by hardships on the mountain, I was just a broke writer when I returned. Now, what was that lesson I learned? How had I grown? It was like watching a snake slide out of its old skin, leaving it behind. We who dare to leave it behind—we who would rather eat the fruit of enlightenment from the gutter than the rotten feast of kings—are the new sages. We are the new skin of the old serpent and our enlightenment would be found wherever we sat. Whether in prison, on Skid Row, or in the Humboldt hills, we would find it, because we knew it was everywhere.

Goldie let me stay at her place as often as I

wanted and the pallid, yet complementary tone of the room full of books, odd trinkets, and thrift store fashion gems festooned my visual expanse. It was a great place for writing. My time in Seattle was coming to an end, or so I thought, as I planned my way back down to LA. I needed to retrieve the Gnostic Rocket from Albert and Macy and sell it for cash so I could pay for school and buy myself a couple of months of financial breathing room in order to resettle.

I picked up a train ticket down to LA and my pals from back in the day had volunteered to put me up while I was there. These two were something else. Tahoe and Hank were twin brothers, not identical, but twins nonetheless. Both of them were geniuses: Tahoe, the rocket company exec, and Hank, the criminally insane. The two brothers were so inseparable that at times they seemed like the same person, but one thing was certain; between these two, a serious amount of fun could be had. As my time with Goldie wrapped up, she began to fluctuate more violently between childish jealousy and calm, faux maturity. She pined for that future long ahead where we were both cloistered away in some beat down Southeast Asian bungalow, writing and fucking and fighting. She'd light a cigarette and call me an asshole, and I'd sit and brood like a berated teen who'd been caught with porn. These were the kinds of visions she put in my head, a kind of monastic camaraderie, a spiritual buddy comedy with lots of graphic con-

Clear Golden Light

tent; one in which we were alone and hidden from the world, but together. And this was a romantic thought that always pervaded my thoughts any time I thought of real romance.

On our last day together, Goldie took me to the Value Village and I picked out a tweed jacket for myself. It fit like a glove. As we walked out of the store, an older woman flagged us and blurted out a joyful hello to Goldie. I stood there like a lurching grey lumberjack in tweed, silently participating in the clucking banter, until we were finally set free to carry on. As we continued, we bumped into my friend Indigo Dave, who had become a famous rock star and also happened to be a former lover of Goldie's. He looked at me, perplexed, "you two know each other?" "No, he just sleeps at my apartment and I make him tea", Goldie replied. She left us to catch up and we both waved her off. I read Dave's tarot for him, "It's your day in the sun, Dave", I said as I pulled out a fantastic set of cards in his favor. His sapphire eyes were captivating and bore down with innocence at the reading. He hung on my every word. I read for the others at the table and excused myself. Dave knew I was broke and slipped me twenty bucks and we shook hands in goodbye, "Here's for the reading, brother".

I found Goldie and she took me to dinner at a French place called Presse, where we ate cheese and drank wine. Neither of us could say no once the drinks started flowing, so we polished off a bottle and a half together and staggered home. The

I-love-yous flowed over me like streams of wine, but my heart was deaf. There was too much tension in my heart and not enough space and time, not enough peace and quiet, not enough safety to cobble a love out of what we had. I told her I loved her back, because I did. In truth, I never stop loving anyone that I invest intimacy in; it just changes.

We sex-wrestled all night and not much sleep was granted. She was a violent lover and would always leave my dick sore from the fucking. But who was I to complain? When I awoke she walked me to the station and we said our goodbyes. She handed me a brown paper bag. The contents were as follows: one bag of hand made sausages from an artisanal Italian sausage maker; one large bottle of San Pelligrino sparkling water; one wisdom tooth; one set of gold cufflinks; one pair of delicately scented underwear; one bag of veggie crisps; two mini bottles of vodka. She kissed me and said, "I love you, fucker", and on the train I went.

¶

*Sudden it comes,
burns, dies,
thrown out.*

I CHING, HEXAGRAM 30, LINE 4

Chapter 19

BECAUSE I DIDN'T HAVE ENOUGH MONEY to pay for the ticket myself, my brother bought it for me. He knew the dire straits I was in and made the kind gesture in order to help me out. As the train left the station, I began to do the final edit of my third book. The train was an experience unto itself; for about the same money as the greyhound bus, I was able to stretch out, walk from car to car, and buy wine (if only I had money). The only cash I had on me was the twenty Dave had given me the day before, and I was not sure how long that cash would have to last me. But the day dragged on and I began to get restless. By evening time, I broke down and bought two mini bottles of wine and, at two glasses for a heavy drinker like me, this was barely enough to give me a buzz, except for my lack of food.

The train sold me on the promise of wifi, but I was to find that this feature was only for people who paid for seats in the sleeper cars. There was nothing, so I wrote and wrote and wrote. Once I was done with the final edit, I put it to rest and began my next book. By the time I made it to the station in LA I had completed 20,000 words, having written at a fevered pace for fourteen hours or so. I was exhausted from the lack of sleep, but in the hour before arrival took a cat-nap. When I came to the station, I grabbed my familiar big brown backpack and typewriter and hauled myself to the inside of the station. With no phone, or internet, I had to trust that I would just see Hank or Tahoe when I arrived, but there was nobody around. I wandered for a bit, then realized that I should look in the bar. Sure enough, there was Hank on drink three, settling his tab. "Hey Hank, it's so good to see you!" "Yeah, you too. Let's get you settled in". We walked to his nondescript Honda and drove to Skid Row.

Last time I had seen Hank, he wasn't with Tahoe, I was still married to Betty, and we all drank together. After we finished four bottles of wine together, Betty passed out, and Hank and I scampered off to the local strip club with Betty's drunken approval. At the time, Betty and I lived with family on the edge of Compton, and the strip club reflected its sociocultural theme. We were so drunk that we didn't care about the potential bad vibes that peeps in the room were giving us, being the out-of-place fellows in an otherwise Afro-American-populated room. Aside from the oddness of our surroundings, the strippers were not our style, so Hank offered to drive us to another

Sudden it Comes

place. Hank and I proceeded to spend the entire night visiting clubs and watching girls dance. It was nice, but I wanted to get home and get some sleep. Tahoe, who was not there at the time, made enough money at his job to bankroll Hank's gutter-friendly lifestyle and there was cash to spare. Through a series of miracles we made it back to the Four Seasons, where they had a suite and I passed out on the floor. In the morning, Hank told me I snored. "Dude, you sounded like creaking wood, and I couldn't sleep till I imagined that I was on a swaying pirate ship, then I slept just fine". It took me four hours after that to get Hank to drive me back to the house with a hungover and pissed-off Betty waiting for me. Hank insisted on bringing a twelve-pack of Miller and sitting down for a drink. Hank didn't leave until dark and Betty was beyond pissed at me, but nothing I did would get Hank to leave, including outright telling him he needed to go. This was Hank's way, master the inertia of the moment till excess is in the rearview mirror, and then go until the cops are called. But that was dirty Hank a good eight months ago, and I thought that maybe his time in the new digs in Santee Court in DTLA would chill him out, especially since Tahoe was all business.

Hank and Tahoe had an agreement as brothers, Tahoe would be the responsible one, pay the bills, keep the money coming in, and keep them in a three-thousand dollar per month apartment in the juxtaposed Skid Row condos. Hank, on the other hand, was to handle the arrangement of getting girls, drugs, drink, and general party planning. It was a good set up for Hank, because he was a total degenerate fuckup. He was a Janus-faced personality: his sober mind was as genius as his brother's, but when he had any kind of substance, upper or downer, he became hard to handle. As far as I knew, he had quit drinking since last I saw him, so I was a bit surprised to find him at the bar when I got into town. It just so happened he decided to resume drinking in my honor.

But wisdom he had and it spilled out at random. As we pulled into the parking garage, he blurted out, "The Sufi consider patience to be a life power, a spiritual power, and the most foundational virtue that one can have. For it is a cross upon which the patient one is crucified. And as resurrection follows crucifixion, so all success and happiness must follow the trying moments of patience". I grabbed my bag and followed Hank through what looked like a fucking third world country. We passed bum after bum and tent after tent, right on the sidewalk in downtown LA. It was awful. And as ugly as that scene was, we made our way to Santee Court in the garment district and were instantly surrounded by Angelino royalty, the financial elite of LA, whose beauty and fitness were the finest that money could buy. The condo complex was populated by gay movie producers, supermodels, new money tech types, and of course Hank and Tahoe.

Sudden it Comes

As I walked in, the rusted lights of dusk flooded the industrial themed room. It was vast and perfect in its design. The entire complex used to be a garment factory and had been converted to ludicrously priced condos complete with Jacuzzi, rooftop pool, gymnasium, and a concierge service. A Japanese-style futon was ornately positioned near the entrance of the apartment. This was to be my home until further notice. No sooner did I drop my bag did Hank hand me a Pabst Blue Ribbon. Now while I'm okay with cheap beer, I hate PBR, but I was exhausted and ready to hit the town up right and proper, so down the beer went. I looked around at the place and marveled at its coolness. Tahoe and Hank weren't very good with décor, so there was virtually nothing in the place. I looked through the cupboards and closets and saw a box of medical needles. I didn't say anything about it. "Get cleaned up, we're going out", Hank said as he tossed an empty shotgunned beer into the corner of the room.

"Tahoe had to head to Texas on business", he said as he clicked on the massive screen projetor which covered a whole wall and dual computer screens which were now playing a porn scene of two girls shoving mini-footballs inside of each other. "So he won't be back till next week, but we'll take care of you for as long as you need to stay here". This news put me at ease, because I didn't have a pot to piss in until I could get to Albert and Macy to retrieve my bike. I put all of that out of my mind and opened up my laptop to setup the wifi. In classic tradition I immediately found the wifi address that I knew must be ours. "It's HOOKERSANDBLOW in all caps", Hank muttered as he lit a cigarette.

Every time Hank would yell for us to go, he would open a new beer and toss me one, so it made it hard to leave, but we eventually made it out the door. I had lost even more weight and was getting close to 215 pounds, so I felt really good and light compared to just eight months ago when I was ashamed to leave the house. We first went to this gritty place about six blocks from Santee Court. As we walked in, it looked like a scene from some LA mob movie with fat, suited, slick-haired, middle aged men sitting around the circular bar. Hank bought us both a shot of Jameson and a Guinness; what we called, "Irish handcuffs". Aside from the quickly mounting buzz, the place sucked, so we made our way to the Golden Gopher where Hank opened a tab. We drank and caught up.

Hank had been in Texas for a while and blacked out at a punk show. He had been beaten up by a group of punks for some blurred reason and ended up asleep and bleeding in somebody's living room at four AM. The cops were called and he was now at the mercy of the Texas lawmen, "those cousin-fucking, shit-kicking, jackboot Nazi motherfuckers" as Hank delicately put it. He spent a night in the clink and was due back in Texas for some business of his own with the law. By some miracle,

Sudden it Comes

Hank had never received a felony conviction in his life, but this one could do it and Hank was terrified of spending some time in prison. This ominous fear loomed above his head like the scythe of the grim reaper. His eyes would go wild and he would turn childlike in fright any time a cop came nearby. When the cops found him in that stranger's Texas living room, they finished what the punks had started at the show and beat him till he was unrecognizable the next day. But here we were in DTLA drinking at the world famous Golden Gopher, surrounded by beautiful people and working on what our angle would be. What we told people would be a facsimile of the truth, but much more attractive to anyone with a nice set of legs.

"Check out the gams on her!" "Huh?", I replied. "Gams, baby, gams! You know the long, slender legs of a beautiful woman". "Gams! I'm going to use that word all the time now". I chuckled as I sipped my Johnnie Walker Black. None of our scammy talk was working on the ladies, but I enjoyed the banter and the reliving of some of our best moments. At around 1:30 we made our way back to Santee Court and drank beers on the roof. I looked out on the city, warm even in mid February, and felt the breeze from the ocean, just on the edge of the horizon. The moon hung in the sky like a flashlight through a frosted windshield and the lights from the surrounding skyscrapers reflected each other like a candle-lit hall of mirrors.

I felt the magic of what was to come, a quickening of inspiration, and I knew that somehow I would find a way to navigate the aftermath of the divorce and make my way to the school that I was told I wasn't allowed to go to. That was my mission and I would make it somehow.

I began to be too drunk to be comfortable and, as an expert drinker, I knew exactly where the sweet spot for quitting was, but Hank didn't have a limit. We made our way back down to the apartment from the roof and Hank blasted Pink Floyd's *Live In Pompei* super loud. The walls were solid concrete, so there wasn't really any limit to how loud we could play the tunes. The place was lit only with the giant projector and some blue Christmas lights the guys had strung up. I looked in the fridge hoping for a light snack, but there was nothing in the fridge except of a case of PBR, and nothing in the freezer but a bottle of vodka. I gave up and just laid down, but Hank walked over excitedly, "Dude, c'mere, I gotta show you this video, it's the best I've ever seen". He stopped the Pink Floyd video and played the new one. The screen bloomed to a black and white image of a young, punk girl slinking out of a bathtub and crawling toward the camera; in song, a holy ghost choir sang out, "Oh, you'll believe it when you see it. Evil is a young man's game". Shot after shot was magnificently placed of this girl dancing slow and seductive, being grazed by a riding crop and manhandled by a hand reaching out. She mouthed the words, "I

Sudden it Comes

like to fuck" into the screen. I couldn't deny that it was beautifully shot and the girl was stunning, flashing a scarified pentagram on her back in the scenes. "I met the lead singer of this band at a show they did at the Viper Room. We partied at a the Roosevelt, that spot I'm gonna show you. We had a good time, but then he trifled with me a bit too much, so I had to knock his ass out". And at that, I acknowledge the video's potency and made my way back to what seemed like my dog bed.

I intermittently awoke to the sounds of clanking aluminum cans and the clicking of a keyboard throughout the night. I would fade back to sleep and when I awoke there was Hank hovering over me with a beer in his hand. "How'd you sleep?" He plopped down cross-legged at the end of the futon, spilling beer on my blanket as he fumbled down. "We're almost out of beer, you wanna go get breakfast?" "Sure, Hank". I got up and peed and looked around at the bathroom. The toilet was full of blood and I didn't want to know why, so I didn't ask. "I'm shitting blood. I think I'm dying or something". "Dude, you should get that checked out man". "Yeah, I will, but first we gotta go get some breakfast!" Hank walked into the bathroom, took out some clippers and started randomly cutting his hair in big chunks, turning his hair into a kind of badly-done Russian fashion mullet. "Does it look straight?"

I was dumbfounded by what I was seeing, this strange amalgam of idiocy and genius in the form of Hank, drunk at ten AM on a weekday. I lied and told him his hair looked great so we could get out the door. I was nursing a pretty hefty hangover from the night before and it looked like Hank had been up drinking without getting any sleep. It was then that the first feelings of concern crept into my mind, but I decided to not be a grump about it and to roll with things as they came.

Chapter 20

WE STEPPED OUT INTO THE NAKED DAYLIGHT and hit the cosmopolitan charm of the city. Men and women dressed in power suits, vendors peddling their fabrics and shitty shirts. Cheap sunglasses sold every half block. This was the garment district and it was clear why it was so named. We made our way to a very nice restaurant where the pastries were sold for five and six dollars each. They were ornate works of art and probably tasted like angel farts, but we were there for breakfast and pastries didn't seem like they could cut the froth of PBR residue in our gullets. The server sat us down and Hank told me to get whatever I wanted. I'd been to many a classy place in New York, but this place was right out of the film, *Get Shorty*. Hank ordered the Cæsar salad and I ordered the ham and gruyère crêpes. I stuck to coffee while Hank nursed a mimosa. It's funny, because you find in your everyday life that food is food and sometimes it's better than others, but when you go to a really amazing place, the most banal food can become a mind blowing experience. Such was the nature of the crêpe that I ate. It was like a French kiss from my breakfast.

We settled the tab and walked to the last bar we had been at the night before. It turns out Hank had left his ID there. So we walked in as they opened the doors and Hank ordered a shot of Jameson and a PBR for both of us. The bar tender was really cute and we both bantered at her. "You know my pal here's a writer, he's gonna be the next fucking Henry Chinaski". "Oh really? What you write about there, Mr. Chinaski?" she said with a smile. "I'm about to put out my book about ecstatic states and why they are valuable in regard to our perspective on life and our sense of meaning". "Oh, so it's an easy read then, huh?" Hank laughed. "What are you two handsome devils doing here on a weekday morning?" Hank's hand came slapping down hard on my shoulder, now speaking in a kind of De Niro voice, "My pal here's never seen the Roosevelt Hotel". He paused a second with his jaw in the air, scratching his chin, "So I figured I'd better lettim take a look around. Then maybe some strippers, then maybe some blow. You know, really show this fuckin' guy a good time". I guzzled my beer, thinking that the only way I would be able to tolerate this constantly buffeting tomfoolery was to attain the same spirit that he had assumed.

Hank tipped the lady and we walked out of the bar, drunk by noon. I'd been an LA resident for about six months, but was almost entirely unfa-

Sudden it Comes

miliar with the layout of DTLA, so I just followed Hank as he capered along. He started doing this thing where he would stop for a moment and stand with a vacant gaze like he was having a vision and then would shake his head and growl like a dog, resuming his more normal status of happy drunk. But as we walked, the shots and beers caught up with us and we were more and more intoxicated.

As we walked aimlessly down the street looking for another bar, we came upon a long- haired Mexican fellow who seemed extremely agreeable. He was wearing a Grateful Dead t-shirt and had thick black horn-rimmed glasses. Hank waved the guy down and asked him where a bar was. "Oh yeah, man, there's a good spot like three blocks from here. You just go around this corner to the right and walk three blocks down. They got really cheap beer and free chips and salsa. I think it's called Aqui Es Donde Se Muere". "Cool, man. You wanna join us? I'll buy you a beer". Hank pulled out a thick roll of twenty dollar bills and thoughtlessly waved the money around. "Um, well, yeah man, sure". Hank lurched like a marionette, "I'm Hank and this is my honored guest". "Hey, it's nice to meet you guys. You seem cool, man. My name's Louis. Hey, man are you alright? You seem a little jumpy". Hank had been bobbing his head around like he was stretching for a boxing match and doing a little dance with it. I chimed in, "yeah, he's fine, we've just been drinking for nearly twenty-four hours now". "Oh, okay, well just be cool man, alright?" Hank gave a gold-toothed sneer and a disingenuous smile from ear to ear. We followed Louis into Donde Se Muere and sat down at the bar. Hank slammed a twenty down onto the bar, hard enough to stop the midday drinkers for a moment as he shouted, "tres cerveseas, por favorrr!" The woman, who honestly looked more like a stroller-pushing, overweight Mexican mother than a bartender, popped open the beers, handed them to us, and went back to talking to the other day drinkers in Spanish.

This place was a sight to see; the entire ceiling was bedecked with compact discs hung from the tiles. The air conditioning spun them all around, creating flashes of rainbow light throughout the room like a bunch of disco balls. But as I got caught up in the extreme quaintness of the room, I lost track of Hank, who was now over speaking broken Spanish to a couple of guys who looked like ranchers at the other end of the bar. This kind of thing made me nervous because I had seen that scowl pop up more often as he got further down the drunk hole, and it was this concern that stopped me from disappearing into my own oblivion.

We finished our beers at the Muerte and stepped outside with Louis and I tried to keep conversation with him to put him at ease around the growing hulk that was Hank. As we walked and talked, looking for another place to get a drink, we came to a street corner where Hank stopped and beat his chest like a gorilla, letting out a big "mruaah!",

Sudden it Comes

like he just conquered a mountain peak. Louis jumped back, startled, "Hey, I think I gotta go, man. You should take care of your friend. It was good talking with you". Louis scurried off in a nervous but metered pace while Hank stood with the veins around his eyes bulging as he panted and heaved.

"Dude, you gotta cut that shit out, especially in public. You're liable to attract the attention of the cops". At that, Hank shrunk again like the flinch of a dog that had been beaten by its owner. "Okay, okay man. Um, let's find ourselves a cab and get to the Roosevelt". It was not as easy to hail a cab in LA as it was in New York. Nobody wanted to stop, but I also recognized that Hank was visibly disturbed. We finally got one to take us there. Hollywood is not really that far from downtown, but with Hank in the car, the cab ride was agonizingly long. The cab driver instantly regretted picking us up, and his face was stern. Hank slapped the driver's shoulder, and he flinched at being touched. "Hey brother, you wanna go get some strippers with us later?" The driver looked at me in his rearview mirror, inferring with his eyes I better keep my pal in check. "Dude, don't touch the driver". "Oh yeah, sorry man! I'm just really excited for strippers!" "Are you even gonna be able to get us into the hotel acting like a maniac?" "Yeah, don't worry, my little Padewan, I got you covered". Hank's reassurances did little to comfort me, but I was beholden to him as my benefactor and there was no place to go other than where he took me. I didn't have a working phone, so I couldn't just call Tahoe to tell him Hank needed a talk down. As brothers, they would look out for each other, and during their lives together they had struck a tenuous, but successful balance between glamor and squalor; Tahoe's water to Hank's oil.

We got to the lobby of the Roosevelt Hotel and walked to the counter. Hank had trouble walking straight, but he put on his game face because he knew he wasn't safe to unravel till we got to the room. The erudite and fashionably gay front desk agent checked us in. As he typed in Hank's info, he occasionally looked up at me with stern and worried eyes, but gave us our keys and sent us off. The room was spectacular, with a full bar, two beds and a view of the Hollywood sign. We both plopped onto our beds and just enjoyed the room. Neither of us had had anything to eat except beer and I was getting hungry. I mentioned food, but Hank said he only wanted beer, but would buy me something. He called room service. "Yeah, get me a filet mignon, medium rare with mashed potatoes and asparagus. There, I got you some food, brother". I thanked him and went into the bathroom. I peed with the door open and Hank came in, "Here's a hundred and sixty bucks, just so you have some folding money. Lemme know if you need more". "Thanks Hank!" I told him I needed to stretch my legs and he asked me to go to the front desk for suggestions on good bars on the strip, so I made my way there.

Sudden it Comes

There is a feeling you get when you're in a high roller's hotel room and you got a little money in your pocket. It is like being a king for a day. I made it to the front desk and asked about the bars and the clerk stopped me, "Is your friend okay? He seemed..." the clerk waved his hands and bobbed his head side-to-side, "...a little crazy". "Yeah, I know". I made up something on the fly. "He just got dumped by his girl and is all torn up about it. We figured it might be good to get out and enjoy the clubs". "Well, okay, but make sure he doesn't break anything". "Will do!" I said with a comforting smile as I took the pamphlet they gave out to the people who wanted to party. As I made my way back up to the room, I spied the extravagant bar in the lobby, which boasted a fine scotch selection, stunning bar maids, and a den of leathered chairs that would make Winston Churchill shoot in his pants. I got back just in time for my meal to arrive and Hank was sipping Grey Goose straight from the bottle. The filet mignon was unbelievable and I ate it like the ravished hunger beast I was. "Fuckin' good right?" "Oh yeah" I muttered with a mouth full of potato.

As is often the case after a stunning meal, one is too full to drink. This was a problem because Hank wasn't. As far as I knew, he hadn't had anything but the salad at the French place, but it was now seven PM. When my meal was complete, I told Hank I was going to go get myself a new t-shirt, since everything I owned was quite ragged after the months in the wilderness. Hank said he'd hang back, but I didn't really care what he was going to do. I just needed to get away from him for a bit. I walked down the strip and popped into a Hipster-Fuck Apparel shop, where a skinny girl in a black wife beater greeted me; her braless breasts poking out under the tight top. She had a black beanie on her head and a thin, rap-mogul-style gold chain around her neck. "Welcome to Hipster-Fuck-Apparel, lemme know if you need any help", she said with an unconvincing smile. I looked around at all the shirts and found a black v-neck. All of my clothes were from fifty pounds ago, and I looked like a crack-head in my present threads. I hazarded to try a large and it fit perfectly. It's embarrassing to say, but I finally felt beautiful again. I paid the fine young lady and wandered back to the Roosevelt and up to the room. Dropping my shopping bag on the floor of the room, I changed into the v-neck and fixed my hair in the mirror.

Hank was watching pay-per-view porn with his pants on and I resigned myself to visiting the bar in the lobby. I told Hank my plans and scampered down the hallway, looking to cure that fine steak with some single malt. I settled in on one of the tufted leather lounge chairs and awaited the bar maid. She came up to me and asked what I wanted, "I'll have a Laphroaig with a single ice cube. And could you keep an eye on me, it won't be long before I want another". "You've got it sweetie". I watched her walk away and I knew why she was

Sudden it Comes

there. Speaking in the most base of terms, she was that elusive mix between erudite queen and craven porn star that drives men to madness. Her flirtation was spot on in a way that made you think there might actually be a chance for love. She came back with my drink and a wink and told me she'd be back soon. Everything done in LA is done to further one's own agenda. I knew this about her and everyone else, but I didn't care. Hank had made his way to the bar as well and was chatting up a stunningly handsome man in a bespoke suit. You could crack an egg on his jawline. "I'm meeting this bitch here that I've been dating. Dude you should see her titties". I immediately lost interest in the guy. "Yeah, she went to the best plastic surgeon in LA and man, you can really tell the difference!" Hank nodded in approval as he slugged his Heinekin. "What are you drinking, man, lemme buy you another. Dude, what's in your glass?" "I'm having a Laphroaig, but I was thinking that Macallan eighteen-year looks pretty nice". In Hank's De Niro voice he blurted, "Hey barkeep, three Heinekins, a Macallan 18, neat, and wha, what are you having, bro?" Titty guy, quipped, "I'll have a Belvedere on the rocks with a lemon". "Classy choice" I replied. We all swilled our drinks, but the conversation was not to my taste. I had been spending my spare time talking about consciousness, increasing spiritual awareness, and personal improvement, and here I was in the presence of two men who epitomized misogyny. But I was no angel either, fawning over the bar maid and trying to make her laugh at every turn. I didn't want to marry her, so in a way the judgments I made on Hank and Titties were unfair. I was along for the dick joke ride as well.

Titty guy's girlfriend showed up, and she was as beautiful as he crassly described. I was embarrassed of my ruddy condition and even more concerned about Hank, but it seemed that he actually thrived as long as he wasn't left to himself; that's when the scowling and threats of violence would emerge.

I went and lounged again on the tufted chair and Hank came over. I stared up at the ceiling and Hank slung his leg over mine like lovers might. "Look at this gorgeous ceiling, brother. This is how we all fit". He pointed up at the designs, "See how you are that mandala and I am that frame around you? I want you to know that I support what you are doing. It's God's work, what you're doing. Remember that when times are hard. But you know what, you don't have to worry about that because Tahoe and I are gonna take care of you. You can stay with us as long as you like and you can make sure I don't drink all the time. I need you, man, I need your goodness. Tahoe isn't enough. I need you here with me, brother".

As I lay there with Hank, my barmaid came by, "Hey guys, there are lots of people watching and I don't want to get in trouble". She looked at Hank, "You're making people nervous". "Ok, we'll head

Sudden it Comes

out, thanks for the heads up". We walked out onto the strip and just started walking, but we made it less than a block before Hank just stood on the sidewalk, looking like a zombie. He didn't respond to me and the people walking by kept a wide berth from him. "Hank! Hank! Dude, you're scaring people". He just looked up at me with his head down and his eye fixed like lasers on me, a sneer on his lips, revealing his gold tooth. I coaxed him down the street like a zoo keeper tending to a hungry lion, his frazzled energy like sparks flinging from a tesla coil. I didn't really know where to go, so I got him to double back with me to the room so we could regroup.

Chapter 21

BACK UP IN THE ROOM HE STAGGERED AND groaned like a hobo and began talking shit to me, "Hey, WHORE, why don't you fix me another drink before I fuck that mouth of yours?" I slapped the back of his head and he head-butted me so hard that my vision went white. The scent of chlorine filled my nose as I reeled from the hit. "Jesus, Hank, chill out man!" "Don't trifle me you fucking whore, now lets get some girls". "No, seriously man, I'm not here to be your whore, I'm your friend and as thankful as I am for all this, I will not be subject to abuse!" Hank softened shamefully and put his hand against my neck as I held my nose, waiting for blood. He put his other hand under my chin and raised it for inspection, looking at my nose. "You okay man?" "No, I'm not okay, you just fucking head-butted me!" "Oh shit, I'm sorry man..." He stumbled over to the Grey Goose bottle that was now half empty, "lemme pour you a drink, okay? Is that okay?" "Brother, all of this...", he waved his hands around at the room with a sway in his gait, "...is for you. I know you've had it rough, brother, and I want to show you that I love you". I morosely acknowledged his apology as he poured the vodka with no regard for ice or mixers. I was really drunk as well and in this space felt a bit more at ease to enjoy the state. As Hank handed me the glass of vodka, I noticed his palm was bleeding down into the sleeve of his shirt.

"Lemme look at that". "Oh shit, I have no idea how that happened!" A patch of flesh the size of a thumb tack had flapped open where the wound was and I took his hand and kissed it. I then held his bleeding hand to my face, then placed his palm to my teeth. I bit the dangled flesh off his hand and swallowed it, "you are my communion, brother". We kissed and our stubble rubbed like sand paper, face to face with open mouths, holding hard like we were fighting for dominance. We fell onto one of the beds and just looked at each other like lovers would. "I love you brother and I won't ever hurt you". Hank said as he held my head with both hands. "I love you too Hank". We got up and I took him into the bathroom to clean up his still bleeding hand. We poured a little vodka on it and resolved to head out again.

We called a cab for pickup in half an hour and went to another bar within the hotel. We slammed two whiskies and spoke madness to anyone around us that would listen. The cab arrived and Hank told the cab driver to take us to the best strip club in LA. "Oh yes, sir, I know the best one for sure.

Sudden it Comes

It's in Beverly Hills. Do you want me to take you gentlemen there?" "Yes!" Hank replied joyfully. "Here's three hundred bucks for the strippers, just tell me if you need more, okay?" "Okay, Hank". It was now 2:30 in the morning and Hank and I walked into a virtually empty strip club. This meant that we were the only paying customers in the room and we were in high demand. Hank found his type almost instantly and disappeared, meanwhile I sat down to watch this black girl dance. She was astonishingly pretty and I couldn't take my eyes off of her. I cried to my self, "Oh, god, oh god, oh god" as she spun around the pole and crept my way with a smile that glowed neon blue from the lights. I was her only customer and she did the whole show for me. I was as stricken as a man can be at that moment and took her to a booth for a lap dance. For every one dance I paid for, she gave me one for free and money was no object, so I put it all on her.

A server came by, "It's impolite not to buy your girl a drink, sir". "Alright, well, what would you like, love?" She took a Heineken, the same as me. "So what's your name?" "I'm Naomi" "Whoah! That's a beautiful name! Do you have a boyfriend, Naomi?" "No, I don't. So tell me about yourself". My grin was Cheshire and I spilled the details of what I had been doing, writing about psychedelics, going on a journey of enlightenment, and so on. All of these details seemed to genuinely interest Naomi and she ate up my words like an eager pupil. "My cousin tried something called DMT and he said he saw God. He totally changed what he was about after that". I lit up like fireworks, "Yeah, yeah! That's exactly it! Now it's not what I would say seeing God, but it is a life-changing experience. You should try it when you get the chance. Maybe if you hang out with me when you're off duty here I can show you?" Naomi's big brown eyes widened with a soft grace one might not expect from a Beverly Hills stripper, "I'd like that a lot".

I didn't see Hank until five AM and we left with our respective stripper's phone numbers. "We got stripper girlfriends!" Hank said happily. A cab was waiting for us outside and it took us back to the Roosevelt where we stumbled into our room and passed out. When I awoke around eleven AM, the room was a shambles and my head hurt so bad. Hank was already up and looked like the night had finally taken the piss out of him, or so I desperately hoped. "Do we need to go check out or anything?" "Nah, I just paid for one night, so we can just leave. Let's go get some breakfast downstairs and head back to our place". "Sure, Hank".

At breakfast, I had bacon and eggs while Hank drank vodka sodas. I knew we couldn't stay in any one place for more than a couple of minutes before drawing unwanted attention and sure enough, the bad vibes continued. We made it to a cab unscathed but upset another cab driver on the way home. Somehow, Hank had managed to convince

Sudden it Comes

some girl from his dating app to meet up with him later, so though he was totally blotto, I still had to spackle him together for another evening of revelry. By this point I was absolutely exhausted and had lost any desire to drink, or do anything other than try to get my important documents from Betty so I could sell my bike. When we got back, I told Hank I need more sleep and plopped down on the floor to sleep. Hank turned on the Pink Floyd in Pompeii video once again and let it blare as he drank beer after beer. I tried to sleep, but it was useless, so I opened my laptop and talked with my friend Dr. August. The good doctor and I had been friends on social media for about a year and we hung out with each other when he was in LA, when we spoke at the same conference.

I had been flirting online with Shawn, this little rock and roll woman who lived in South Carolina. She had lived in New York the same time as me and even in the same neighborhood, but we never bumped into each other despite having similar connections. She took a liking to my wit and we had been exchanging messages here and there as my internet access would dictate. I totally considered her to be out of my league, at least by way of looks, but I persisted in trying to charm her. It is a fault, or benefit, of my character that I am in love with love itself. I am brightest when I am held to its livening flame and when its potential for greatness blooms before me. I am not one for solitude, though over my time in the Humboldt hills learned to use it to my advantage. Shawn to me was a shiny object in the murky waters of my mind, a focal point and breath of potentiality that I would use as a ploy to be productive. But we had been flirting for a couple of weeks and talked nearly every day, and as long as she would entertain my advances, I would be game for it. As I clacked away at my laptop, Hank opened the fridge for a beer, "Hey do you think I could do that DMT? You were saying your friends Albert and Macy had some. Would they be willing to share some?" "Yeah man, I'll ask Albert and see what's up". I wrote to Albert and sure enough they agreed to meet with us the next day at their place. I was bummed because I hadn't gotten my mail and documents from Betty, so I wouldn't be able to pick up my bike, without which I was a sitting duck.

I was really fucking exhausted by the onslaught of Hank and was wearing thinner and thinner in my patience with his demons. He asked me to join him at this bar called Redwood to meet a girl from the dating app he was using and I hesitantly agreed. I typed up some poetry on my vintage typewriter and showed it to Hank. "Man, this is soo good, dude! What's this new book you're working on?" I adjusted myself as I sat, a bit perplexed and stymied, "I thought I knew. I thought it would be about finding enlightenment in the woods, but I don't know if I'm any better off than I was when I left LA last fall. I don't feel any more enlightened, or wise, just further down the road, I

Sudden it Comes

guess. Can I read you some of it?" "Yeah, please, please!" I recited the tale of how I felt in those first few days alone without the comfort of home, with the whole world pissed off at me and how low I felt, but also about the newfound strength I had after taking the chance. "Oh my god, dude, I remember when I rode my bicycle from Seattle to San Francisco with a big backpack. I remember it started raining and I didn't have any place to go. I wasn't even near a rest stop. I pulled off the road enough to not be seen and curled up at the base of a tree, soaking wet. I thought I was going to die of hypothermia, but I shivered, cold and wet through that night and I saw the morning come. I didn't get much sleep, but when I did wake, the clouds were gone and the light shone through the trees like a spotlight. The dew was glistening everywhere and I felt more motherfucking alive than I had ever felt before. Nobody understands what it is we are capable of, because they don't know what its like to die in the cold and live again". "Hank, that was beautiful". He hovered over me with perhaps the deepest sincerity I'd seen in a long while, and I saw the man peek out from within the beast.

We made our way to Redwood and met up with the girl and a friend of hers. I said hello and Hank sat beside her. Her name was Dolores, and despite her unfortunate name, she was a charming Scottish woman whose penchant for swearing and talking dirty was very alluring. Hank, on the other hand was uncharacteristically quiet. He could hardly articulate anything at all and sat beside Dolores, nearly catatonic. I held up the conversation and talked him up, but it felt like I was doing promotions at a wax museum. Hank was more like an abandoned Romanian baby than the dick-swinging reprobate he made himself out to be. After a couple of hours of awkwardness, we left the place and walked to another spot ten blocks down the road. I asked what happened and he began to snarl like an orc every time I tried to talk to him. So I just walked beside this demon man whose shadow had outgrown his light and tried my best to let what love I could share to be his. "She fucking liked you better, man. I fucked it up, I couldn't say a fucking word. I was just too nervous", he muttered again, more quietly to himself, "too nervous...and I just...mruahhhhhhh!" He flailed his arms out and back behind himself, his head flung forward like a vulture, exuding evil like a Satanic power station. I had, over the course of the last couple of days, been able to keep the demon at bay, but there was no containing it. Something was deeply wrong, and it could not be corrected by a drunk and confused me.

We almost made it to another spot when he began to shake his head like a mental patient, growling among the crowded street folk. I pulled him by his arm to try to coax him away from harm. "Don't fucking touch me! You think you're better than me, motherfucker?" "Well, at this moment I am", and as soon as I said it, Hank swung his fist

Sudden it Comes

to the side of my head knocking me sideways but not out or over. And before he could swing again, a bicycle cop who had doubtlessly been following us for a block or two came down upon us quickly, "Hey, get away from that man!" the cop yelled as he jumped off his bike. Hank leapt up like a frightened cat with eyes like saucers and shrunk back like a vampire. "It's okay, it's okay! He was just playing around with me, *right Hank*?" I looked in his feral eyes. "Right?" "Yeah, officer, I'm sorry, I'm sorry". Hank whimpered. "Listen, you gotta get this guy home. If I see him again, he's spending the night in jail". "Okay officer, thank you", I said, trying to comfort Hank, who was now almost clinging to me like a refugee.

He was shaking with fear, "You gotta get me home right now man, you don't understand the jackboot. Have you ever had a cop put his boot on your face and stand on it? You ever looked up at one of them pieces of shit while they take pleasure in beating you minutes from life? You gotta get me home, you gotta get me home". I tried to calm him with my award winning levity, my arm over his shoulder. "Well Hank, maybe you should stop punching your friends?" "I hit you? Is that why the cop appeared out of nowhere?" I was deeply disturbed by what I had witnessed; in fact the punch to my head was the last thing on my mind. I was legitimately concerned for Hank's life and well-being. To me, there was no way that I could keep drinking with him. I couldn't give him any reason to use me as an excuse.

It was late when we got home and I laid down on my dog bed to get some sleep. Hank went into the other room and closed the door. The rooms were separated, but you could hear everything and I could tell he was on a live video xxx site. I drifted off. I awoke at eight AM with Hank above me with a beer in his hand. He started in a bad Cockney accent. "I find you to be a pretty little thing. Don't I then? Don't I? Don't I find you pretty? So here's what you're gonna do. Just stick that little ass up in the air". Hank's shadow cast long upon the wall, like a vampire huddled over its victim, and in reality his shadow was far bigger than the man who lurched over me. He was sucking the goodness right out of me, then and there. "That's right, just stick it in the air, cause I'd like to fuck it, wouldn't I? Wouldn't I then? Wouldn't I? Like to fuck it?" "Dude, we need girls. This is not working".

I got him to leave me alone and I just laid there quietly for another couple of hours. It was Valentine's day and I was alone, scared, hung-over, broke, and living with a psychopath. This was not my vision of the enlightened path. I began to cry hard, but quietly, so as not to attract Hank's attention. Hank walked into the room, "Hey, I'm gonna get this cam girl to shove three dildos in her pussy, hey? Hey? Brother, what's the matter?" "I MISS MY FAT WIFE, I MISS MY CHILDREN, I MISS BETTY, I DON'T WANNA BE A FUCK UP!" I blurted, sobbing as Hank crouched beside me, having returned to his kinder self. "You had to leave her man, you

Sudden it Comes

didn't love her anymore. You and her were no good any longer. Look what you've done so far. Look at what you're gonna do. You're my hero, man. Don't cry". Hank's eyes got really sad as he began to well up too and he put down his beer and hugged me on the floor. I sobbed into his beer-stained shirt. "Okay, okay". I caught my breath and calmed down. "I know I'm not supposed to be with Betty, I know I'm supposed to get into college and put out my book on consciousness, but I'm just exhausted! I can't drink with you. I can't do it! I don't want it and neither should you. You're one of the smartest people I know and you're fucking up!" "I know, brother, I know, but I'm gonna make it okay. Here, I'm gonna put this beer down, and we're gonna go to see Albert and Macy and I'm gonna do the DMT and it will be okay. Okay?" "Okay, Hank".

"I'm just so lonely, dude, so fucking lonely. These girls don't do it, the beer doesn't do it. I know it wasn't right, but with Betty I was home and now I have no home. I have no home and I don't know when I'm gonna feel like that again. It's why I stayed with her for so long, I was scared to not have a home. That deep love that comes from the very heart of a person. No matter where I've been, I've not been home. That clueless woman is the only place I know, the only safe place I've known. But it's dead. It's fucking dead and I can't bring it back to life, no matter how hard I try. I tried so fucking hard. So fucking hard to bring it back. It's just dead. And now, here I am on your floor, weeping like a bitch because I left a dead life, but it was MY dead life. I don't regret it, but I'm lost without it". I just whimpered and wept with Hank at my feet.

Hank had tears in his eyes. "I need to read you something. It's about me and Jenny":

I cross the street against the light and take the last half block in long strides, cig dangling from my lips, bag of McDonalds in one hand, pack of Marlboro Mediums and a Vitamin Water in the other. This is my classic offering. I wait outside the back alley door in the slight rain, it's not as easy as a text or a call... those lines have all been shut down. I send an email, a couple minutes added delay, cause we are miles apart...time zones... universes. It amazes me that we try to communicate at all, and then I remember that it's not by choice that we are bound together, it's something else. We each have our other ones, hers a loyal boy in a band, a calculated coincidence, slow and careful, quietly cultivated and nursed from seed to sapling over years; mine a stunning blond, a frantic scramble, snatched up midair and blindfolded, all style no substance... my sprint to her jog. When she finally opens the back gate I'm half wet. She pretends she doesn't know the booty shorts and wife beater disheveled look is how I like her best, complains that she looks terrible, but inside she is smiling at my racing heart.

Sudden it Comes

Her small apartment is cluttered with the ruins and wreckage of our old love, and sprinkled with the monuments and hidden treasures of her new one. I concentrate on pulling out a smoke. Block it all out with that first drag. We sit and smoke. Most days that's about it, we share a couple cigs and we say a couple words and I'm gone, but not today. Today with each smoke we drift a little closer. Today each word is spoken a little quieter. The distance between us is halved and the attraction is more than doubled. We both fight as hard as we can...or maybe it's just me fighting it, maybe she is toying with me, making sure she still has the card to play. A little closer and it doesn't matter who has what card, we are in each other's arms, and oh fuck it's like the first breath of air I've had in months. It's the only thing we have left after all the betrayal, this magnetic force, this brilliant spark that I couldn't reproduce in a million years with a million different girls. It's so hot and so bright, and it goes on getting brighter for what seems like forever, filling up the void in my guts like a god damned supernova... but nothing lasts forever. A spark is just that, it's good for one thing...starting fires", [Hank began to weep profusely] *"and our fire has already burned, it burned hot and it burned up everything in its path. There's nothing left here to burn. The ashes are fertile, good for planting, but I ain't Johnny fuckin' Appleseed, that's drummer boy, so I get dressed, light another smoke and hit the door".*

And there we were, two tough guys who had faced the threat, ran the drugs, tried the scary things and came inches from death on many occasions, but now we were dancing with insanity and crying as those who mourn for we had seen the death of love.

Chapter 22

WE CLEANED OURSELVES UP AND HEADED TO see Albert and Macy for Hank's first experience with DMT. Hank was not in ideal condition for this kind of thing, but it was the only chance we would have in a long time, so I put my trust in the machine elves. When we arrived, Albert and Macy were in classic condition; Albert was working on making a geodesic dome and Macy was helping him. They stopped to greet us. I had told them about Hank, how he was smart, but also a bit on the unstable side. We walked in and got down to business. They had just ordered a pizza and they offered us each a slice and a beer. Hank didn't seem drunk at all, but after four days of drinking with him, it was hard to tell what was what. We sat Hank down on the couch in front of Albert's fireplace and I talked Hank through it all while Albert prepared the goods. He sat and meditated for a moment, or whatever kind of mindfulness he could muster, and indicated he was ready.

Albert held the DMT-loaded dabs bong, lit it up, and held it for Hank to inhale upon. He pulled it in and held it and held it and held it until we all got nervous he would never breathe again. Hank shook with a shudder and flopped his legs all over and began to make burping noises like he was going to vomit. DMT is dissociative, so Hank was not aware of his body. But he whimpered and moaned and vomited on himself. Albert and Macy both looked gravely concerned and cleaned him off. He began to slump sideways like he was trying to move, but he had no motor skills due to the effects of the substance. He ended up slumped in my arms, cradled like a baby, and whimpering desperately, flopping his arms like a puppet.

When he came to he just sat there silently. "How you feeling, buddy, are you coming back?" "Oh my god, oh my god, oh my god". "Hey Hank, Hank...Hank...you there, buddy?" He finally opened his eyes and I helped him back onto the couch. He just sat there stunned. "I can't believe it! What the holy fuck? I was in the center of all things and was being ripped apart, like I was being punished; I didn't want to be pulled apart", Hank said with a stony gaze. "Can I do it again? I didn't get, um, I...I was being shown something... It...Can I do it again?" Albert looked me with a surprised and disturbed smile, "Yeah, sure man... I mean, are you sure you're okay? You like barfed and stuff. We held you like a baby". "Oh man, I'm sorry, no, yeah, I'm okay, I just need to see some-

Sudden it Comes

thing. Can I do it again?" Albert nursed the inhalation to Hank once again and once again the results were similar with whimpering and moaning, like he was having a nightmare. When he came to, he just sat there, stunned and unable to articulate anything. "I can feel the buzzing in my head, like bees. It feels like there's bees in there. It was like I was being destroyed and the bees were putting me into infinitesimal pieces".

When he was ready, we stood him up and let him have a beer. Albert, Macy, and I had never seen a DMT trip like that. After we hung out for a bit, I thought it would be good to get Hank back home since we still had ample time for him to sober up before his miraculous second date with Dolores.

As we drove back to Santee Court, Hank kept blurting out, "you didn't tell me it would keep happening after it was over. It's still here. They are still here. The Void, the fucking VOID is here". I laughed, "Yeah, well you can fool people, but the psychedelics will mercilessly show you when you are fucking up, and you are fucking up". Hank shook his head madly like a psychiatric patient and continued to repeat sentences. When we got back to his place, he stirred like a man on the run, pacing back and forth, gazing at the floor. He was drunk and I was to remain sober, so I had to watch this without any filter. The DMT had punished him. When the elves on the other side got a hold of him, they let him know what the dissolution of self looked like when it was done by force. I was terrified by what he described, the lack of existence itself, the divine spark being snuffed out—for what? Shitty behavior? An unrealized potential? I sat and wrote and tried to let my levity increase, but I was tense. Hank's energy was so intense it was nearly visible, and I couldn't stand the sight of it.

I messaged Dr. August online:

"I've been drunk babysitting a rocket-scientist Charles Manson".

"Hey, the lows make our highs higher, right? Saturn is kicking our Leo asses right now. Bringing his depressing weight to bear. Alchemically he is lead, the opposite of the sun's gold".

"Should I make a salute to Saturn to ask for mercy?"

"Yes, salute to Saturn for sure. May he give us patience and endurance".

"Any snappy phrases I can throw its way?"

"Old bastard comes to mind".

"I'm gonna make a massive sigil. I have some poison I need to gift to Saturn. I made a star that included the pentacle and pentagram; the sacred union".

"Well here's what you should write on it. *Lift the weight from my royal light.* We're eternal optimists, even in the midst of shit. But we just need a little attention to help us through, to know we have meaning and value beyond ourselves. Saturn isn't all bad, he gives us endurance. Gravity. With-

Sudden it Comes

out gravity, the sun is nothing".

"Agreed! It's handy to have an astrological master at my disposal. Thank you for your advice homey. So what's in the charts for us?"

"Well, a few bumps and ongoing tensions, but April is the real shit storm. Mars enters retrograde in March so this will fuck with general energy and motivation. But I think we just need to get to the bottom of our hearts and find our value in and of ourselves. I'm getting there, but I'm not out of the woods yet. We are our universe and yet we seek outside of ourselves for love, pleasure, power. Most people do. But as initiates, we should know better. This is how you break down the duality".

"I've been trying to live with the pain and allow it to exist rather than seek something to cover it up, but that proves easier said than done".

"Yes, the pain hides the lesson that we need in order to grow. I've been trying, too. If I had women around, I'd be distracting myself from my self. No doubt about it".

After Hank left the condo to go on his date with Dolores, I took Dr. August's advice and created a sigil. For those who are unaware, a sigil is made through the magical application of writing where you manipulate the words of your intentions into symbols. The idea behind this is that the archaic aspects of our mind, which has a much more hearty penchant for accepting magic, faith, etc., responds better to symbols and not words. Therefore, the symbols are created using the letters of intention, broken down into an image. The subconscious works on this intention long after what you had written the sigil for is forgotten; so as the saying goes, "be careful what you wish for". Practitioners of magic use this method because it is easy, powerful, and fun.

The concrete floor of Hank and Tahoe's condo served as a beautiful, open space for creating my sigil. I drew out a large circle, nearly six feet in diameter; within it I placed symbols that have meaning and power for me, and drew an image of Saturn. I drew a ten-point star which represents the marriage of the Saturnine and Venusian, a blessed union which should lead to balance. In breaking with tradition, I wrote the phrase, *Lift the weight from my royal light* within the circle, as Dr. August suggested. I then mustered all of my sadness, loss, pain, and sorrow until I was crying once more and let the tears fall upon the sigil. I then came on the sigil while staring at it and banished it with laughter. When all was done I cleaned the image from the floor and hoped that all of this pain and frustration was going to come to an end soon, but how it came to be was most strange and horrible.

Chapter 23

I HAD SOBERLY SAT MY WAY THROUGH Valentine's day and was feeling rather glum. I was exhausted; having only slept a handful of hours in the previous four days , I was unable to do anything other than write like my hair was on fire. So I wrote and wrote until Hank burst through the door with a twenty-four pack of beer and Dolores in tow. Both of them were smashed and rowdy. I had been as chaste as a librarian for the day and was not excited to be exposed to this bullshit. But I had no choice, so I let it happen. Dolores greeted me with a hello and pulled out a bag of cocaine, emptying its contents onto the granite countertop. Meanwhile Hank went digging in the closet and presented the box of needles that I discovered the day I arrived. Dolores sniffed up two lines as fast as she could and turned around rubbing her nose asking Hank what he was doing. "Oh no, dude! I can't be here for this, man. I can't be here for this. Please don't do this in front of me, Hank!" I said pleadingly. You see, a mutual friend of ours—

Dylan, Hank's best friend—had died of a heroin overdose in New York. He died in Hanks arms. When I previously asked Hank about that day, he said, "The meat wagon showed up to get Dylan's body and they zipped him up in a body bag. We were on the fifth floor and they started dragging his body down the stairs, letting his lead thump on every stair. I stopped them and picked up his body and carried it down to the meat wagon. I couldn't believe it, I saw him die and I watched them take his body". This was my experience with needles and I had zero tolerance for it and so I plead with Hank not to shoot up in front of me.

Hank exploded in anger at me, "What the Fuck? Why are you doing this to me? I'm exercising my free will! Why are you making me not do this? I do what I fucking want!" Dolores became visibly concerned and doubled back, astonished at Hank's response. He had taken his shirt off in order to give himself an injection; he had no intention of not shooting up. "Hank, I can't watch this shit and I don't want to find your body first thing in the morning. Don't ask me to do that". "Shut the fuck up you fucking whore. I've given you everything I have, spent thousands of dollars on you and this is how you fucking treat me?" He now had taken a fighting stance to me and screamed with purple-faced indignity, "GET THE FUCK OUT OF MY HOUSE BEFORE I KILL YOU, YOU MOTHERFUCKER!" This had all happened in a matter of a minute from the time Hank burst in till now. I was in pajamas

Sudden it Comes

and had my things strewn all over the place. He grabbed my laptop, which had my finished, but unpublished book, as well as the latest contents of my next book. I shuddered at the thought. "I'll throw your shit out of this fucking window right now if you don't get the fuck out of here". Hank's shadow now had complete control and there was no human left to reason with. I pleaded with him to just let me get pants and a coat on and to take my laptop with me as he raged like a maniac and he growled and screamed. Dolores grabbed her purse and put the remains of the coke bag back in her purse and started to make her way for the door. "Now you're making her leave! I'll fucking kill you! I'll fucking kill you!" Dolores got out the door and out of sight. I finally had pants on and took my laptop and charger, a jacket and my shoulder bag. "All of your shit is going out this window. ALL OF IT!" I ran out of the door in a hurry and he slammed it behind me.

As I made my way to the elevator, Dolores was waiting for it. We both hurried inside. "Oh my god? Is he totally insane?" "He's pissed at me about not being able to shoot up in front of me". "Am I safe with him?" I was shaking with adrenaline and desperately trying to come up with a plan. "I'm sorry, I'm sorry, but no, you're fine; women are what keep him content and happy. If you go back to him you will be okay. That's *if* you want to go back". "I want to go back up and make sure he's okay. I think I can calm him down". "I don't know what I'm gonna do. He said he was going to throw my shit out the window. Everything I own is up there except for my laptop, which he almost threw out of the window. I have nothing, no money, no place to go, nothing". Dolores pulled some cash from the purse, "Here's nine dollars, it's all the cash I have. I'm so sorry this is happening to you. Do you want me to leave with you?" "Thank you, but no, you should go back up there. I mean it sounds like you want to". "Yeah, I do. I really like Hank, he was so funny and nice this whole night and then this. I feel like I should give him one more chance". "Okay, well I gotta try to get somewhere that has internet now. Be safe, Dolores". "You too".

I walked out into Skid Row where dozens of homeless people lived just under the lights of Hank and Tahoe's apartment and now I was one of them. At 12:30 at night on Valentine's day, there was nobody who would answer a phone, nobody who would come get me. And with a miraculous nine dollars, I made my way through DTLA looking for a place that had an internet connection. After about an hour of searching, I came upon a twenty-four hour café and made my way inside. This was in the same area as many of the most popular downtown clubs, so the streets were full of partygoers, lovers, and the homeless. I ordered a coffee and decided that I would settle in there for the night and unless rescued, would simply stay awake until dawn at this twenty-four hour café.

Sudden it Comes

Once I found an outlet for my laptop I had to stay plugged in there, lest somebody come along and steal my spot, forcing me to buy another coffee. I needed to conserve what little cash I had because I had no idea what might happen next. It was 1:45 in the morning and I reached out Dr. August, hoping just to get some kind of good human response. Since he was in Australia, he was just getting his day started, so I messaged him once again:

"I'm on the streets tonight. Send me good juju".

"Alright. Shall do".

"My benefactor decided to relapse into IV drug use and when I said I couldn't be around it he went berserk. At first he wouldn't let me leave, then he threw me out. All I could think about is that my work would be lost if he destroyed my computer".

"Shit. Yeah. Work is precious. Our livelihood. Are you okay? Can you stay with someone?"

"I have five dollars and I've just found a twenty-four hour café to drink coffee till dawn. Hopefully my friend will come and get me to a safe spot. I called but nobody answered. No phone. No text".

"Bugger. Okay".

"The problem is staying awake till eight AM. And off the streets. I'm in downtown LA. Crack and heroin and robbery".

"Jesus".

"And people named Jesus".

"Well stay safe my friend!"

"Seriously, I'm so close to giving up on all of this and working as a slave at the big airplane company in Seattle where at least motherfuckers don't try to hurt you. I was reading a book when he barged in. I won't though. My work is too important. My tarot cards say it's going to be a shit sandwich, but I'll be okay".

"Yeah and you can weave all this crazy life shit into it. Give it edge. Make sure you upload your work to Gmail or something as backup. Because it's fucking brilliant brother".

"I have to walk back near the building to see if my shit was thrown out the window as he threatened. My passport is in a bag that's still up there. I've been assaulted three times in the last fou days.

"Yeah go get your shit. Will he cool off?"

"Yes, he will. He fluctuates between extreme anger and sadness. Maybe he'll nod off. I'm gonna be fine, but if not, you are gonna publish my stuff for me, right? Haha!"

"I'll make sure you live on in glory".

"He's with a girl. They are shooting such cool drugs, I'm sure. Thumbs down".

"Sounds like he's in a well of pain".

"I told him there is a dead animal in his well".

"No excuse for being a cunt though".

"It's not like I can't hurt him back, but that is not my purpose. I'm trying to remain true to that purpose. When he's sober, he's amazingly kind and clever. He's been sober about four hours in the last five days though".

"Noble of you".

"I had a nervous breakdown this morning and

Sudden it Comes

he cried too because he knew he was dragging me down with him. I haven't drank anything for two and a half days. I opted out. If I can sell some books I can buy some time until Betty gives me all my mail and shit. She's making me wait till next week and I don't want her to have any idea how dire things have become. I'm two blocks from skid row.

"Keep your balance. Even if the world reels".

"I shall. I might have pissed Saturn off! In other news, I'm talking with a couple about Gnosis. Hah! Must peddle the work of consciousness!"

"Hell yes. Let synchronicity open some doors!"

"Well, I think I just sold a book. I might have to sneak someplace and take a shit. There are no public toilets downtown, or at this café. #hobolife".

"Damn. What about McDonalds? Toilets of the world".

"Also, I'm half hoping my shit was thrown out the window and half not. McDonalds doesn't open till five AM and has no wifi. I want to be out of this situation ASAP, which means I need to ensure I'm connected".

"Yep. Okay".

"It is a sin to human decency that there are not more public toilets".

"It is. Man's gotta shit!"

"If my books went out the window, I can sell them at the bookstore. This is so fucking pitiful. I hope Hank enjoys his drugs. I hear they are so much better than true friends. There's a dumb looking dude in the window eating while his glorious woman shivers".

"That's fucking rough. I think your stuff will be okay".

"Yeah, he's probably crying in the arms of the hot girl he's just finished buttfucking right now. Chivalry is kinda dead".

"No. Sir Gabriel is at hand!"

"I need to go over to Hank's with Robert, who is as big as me, so I can get in and out without threat of violence".

"Yes. Good idea. Shed some clarity".

"My kindness has been mistaken for weakness. I was head-butted in the face the other night".

"Damn. That's gotta hurt".

"Yeah, my nose took most of it, but didn't break. He broke a bone in his hand punching the side of my head too. I do not break easily. Thing is, he promised to pay my coming college bill".

"Is he even able to come good on promises?"

"Depends. Right now it seems like he has a very clear death wish".

"Yep. I wouldn't put up with it just for a shaky promise".

"Once I sell my bike, everything is gravy, or at least manageable".

"Okay. Yeah. You're really flying this tight".

"I can tell everyone good in my life is losing patience. Yeah".

"It's hard for them to understand. People who don't give up everything for freedom".

Sudden it Comes

"Right? They forget I looked for a motherfucking joe job for nine months in LA, to no avail. I feel different now, tougher, even in defeat I exude more power".

"Yes. You know you can still be who you truly are up or down".

"I can't tell if miracles are happening because of grace or because I'm on the right path. How is abuse and druggie bullshit part of the plan?"

"I think the miracles are there to help you through the dark part of the journey".

"My mom emailed me the moment I got wifi. Haven't talked to her in months. First thing she says: 'I send you a hug from god'".

"Thanks mum. And god! I guess it's a nice gesture from her".

"She was kind enough to make the term broad enough to not irk me. I'm getting a nice tired delirium going on. I should be getting visionary soon".

"Yes, let dream and waking merge".

"Right, good time for prognostication. I just want a floor to sleep on for a couple of hours".

"It's the small things".

"On a floor. On anything but the shit smeared sidewalk. I hate when graciousness has strings".

"Hell, I hope you find a king size bed brother".

"It's so surreal. Hank is so generous, then so fucking horrible. He knows it too".

"Yeah those types know how to work our forgiving side".

"I mention it because I was eating filet mignon

at the Roosevelt and drinking Macallan with a girl on my arm a couple of days ago. *And* sleeping in a king size bed. It's funny how I'm the one on the streets and he's the one who is fucked up! Not funny, but you know".

"Embracing extremes".

"He told me I'm noir: I take all the sex and drugs and rock n roll with a nonchalance that is unmatched. I think he misunderstood my tolerance of his rampant assholery as acceptance. I'm so tired. The place promises to be crowded till five-thirty or six AM, so at least I won't be alone. I can understand why homeless people stay awake at night and sleep all day, it's better for safety. But there's that feeling of shame that washes over you when you see dawn's early light creeping over the city and you haven't slept yet".

"Things always look seedier in that light".

"I'm so grateful I found twenty-four hour wifi. I'd be so lost without it".

"Yeah, that's a small miracle right there".

"Everything comes back to ol' Dylan. Sorry, my mind is slipping. I just keep thinking about his song, 'Shelter From the Storm'. I've never in my life been so shit-show and well collected simultaneously".

"It's that balance of extremes again. It's a fine line. Shows it can be done though".

"This all makes me want to go back to the woods and never come back".

"I'm tempted too".

Sudden it Comes

"Hopefully Robert wakes up soon and I can feel safe personally. I'd hate to wait till nine AM to hear him say he will wait till after work to come get me or something. I've run out of options. But I can count four or five miracles. Hank's girl gave me nine dollars. If not for that I wouldn't be able to even have a coffee and wifi".

"That was nice of her".

"Yeah, she offered to take me home with her, but I figured stealing Hank's girl would have been a bad move. God, I keep seeing really exhausted-looking people and then I realize that I'm one of them. A day or two and I'd be stinky and dirty. That's all it takes to fall from grace. Only because I look nice am I even allowed to sit here. At least I have several changes of socks and my fleece blanket. The fleece is integral. Okay, I'm stepping out for a bit. I'll check back in. Thank you for holding me up. I know you have things to do. Wish me luck. I just figured out I can take a bus to Venice and make it easier to get picked up by Robert. If for some reason he isn't available, I have a few other people I can ask for help. The bus should be here in five mintues, so I gotta go. Thank you for holding me up through the night Dr. August. You truly are a better friend from half a world away than a dozen right here".

"Good luck! Stay strong. The darkest hour is before dawn".

I got on a bus to Venice beach and tried my best to get some rest. I was so tired that as soon as I fell asleep, I would snore violently, so I kept waking myself up. I had already been sleep deprived for many days prior, so this all-night stint was the last straw. I didn't know exactly how far along I was, or how long the bus would take, so I couldn't be at ease enough to really invest in sleep. I got off when I recognized the beach area coming up, but undershot it and had to walk a dozen blocks or so. It was just before six AM and even in Southern California, the air was really cold. I pulled the fleece blanket I had grabbed and wrapped myself up in it. I'd like to imagine that at just that moment, Betty drove by and saw a hobo, only to recognize it as her ex-husband. I would grant her that satisfaction.

¶

*Weeping tears
like flowing streams,
sad as if in mourning.
Good fortune.*

I CHING, HEXAGRAM 30, LINE 5

Chapter 24

I MADE MY WAY TO THE BEACH WHERE THERE were lots of people. Venice is cool, but there is a lot of sketchy activity, so I wanted to be where I could be seen. Having a now shut-off smart phone, I had to rely on anything I could get wifi on. I lumbered to a concrete bench and tried to close my eyes, but every time I did, I'd hear a skateboard, or the footsteps of somebody walking by. My state of awareness made everything wiry and electric, like when you take too much Dayquil. I had messaged Robert before I left the twenty-four hour coffee shop, but I hadn't had the chance to see if I got a response from him. There was no wifi on the beach. I sat there on that park bench saying to myself, "How, how...how did this happen? What is going on? Is this how people become homeless?" I couldn't stand sitting there, but I was also terribly lacking in energy, over-caffeinated, and hungry. I looked around at Venice as the sun grew stronger and felt the salty air on my face. I could feel the grit of everything; the ground, the dirty sea, the scabbed drug addicts, the weird Coney Island sadness that sat just under the surface of all I saw, and of course the shame of my own stink.

I still had to take a shit and was averse to the public bathrooms at Venice Beach, so I made my way to a coffee shop that my friend Zeb had taken me to when he came to visit me, months prior.

I got to the spot, but was out of money, having spent the last of it on the bus ride out, so I tried to clean myself up in a shop window and look like I just had a good Valentine's Day. The wifi at the coffee shop was open to the public, so I sat just outside the shop and pirated it. Once I got the internet back up I went inside and snuck into the bathroom. Finally I was able to relieve myself and wash my face in the mirror. I looked like death; white as a sheet and headspun from exhaustion. Robert messaged me and told me he was on his way. He said he'd take care of me, so I waited patiently by the entrance.

Robert was just taller than me, pushing six foot five and had long jet-black hair, a tattooed, muscular build and stunning eyes that were shrouded in ever-present gold Ray-Bans. He always had a serious look on his face and moved with a slow sureness. I nearly wept when I saw him. "Hey buddy, can I get you a coffee?" "Yeah, yes please". He gave me a big hug and we walked in. "Listen, I got stuff to do today, but I'm gonna set you up at the sober house. You can get cleaned up, sleep, and just recover from all this shit. What's the deal with Hank? Is he fucking crazy? The story you messaged me with is nuts!" "Yeah, he was fine and then he would keep turning into this demon man, where Hank wasn't even there". "Jesus, dude, yeah I have people at the sober house who are that way if they drink. It's hard enough to deal with alcoholism, but it's a whole other ballgame when you add mental illness to the mix. It's some fucked up shit".

Robert ran a fifteen-tenant sober house in Venice, whose monthly rent was two thousand dollars per room. All the people who lived in it had to be vetted and interviewed. It was a privilege to pay that much to live there and I was going to stay there for free.

We walked out into the daylight and made it over to Robert's Jaguar. "Dude, sweet ride!" "I know, right? I never thought when I was a junkie that I'd be living in this beautiful place, driving around in a Jaguar! I earn it though. It's not easy dealing with addicts all day long, but I've found that I'm good at it and it's my way of making the world better". "I'm so proud of what you're doing, Robert! Thank you so much for getting me. You saved my ass". "Bro, I would do anything for you. You saved my ass when I was on smack in NYC and had no place to go. I will never forget that, so you just rest easy, get some sleep and I'll come back around later on to take you to dinner". As we pulled up to the house and walked in, he showed me around a bit. He took me to the massive room in the back. It was flush with a great big bed, soft blankets, a bathroom, and a desk to write on. "So Hank still has a bunch of your shit? We'll take care of that tomorrow. For now just get some rest. I got some business to attend to near Betty, you said you needed to get some stuff from her?" "Yeah, she's got my mail and the tabs and license plate for my bike". "Alright, I'll hit her up and get it from her. Sweet dreams, bro".

I took what might have been the most wonderful shower of my life and climbed into bed. I messaged Shawn, who had been privy to the whole scandalous sequence of events. Little did I know what role she might play as things soon changed once again. I fell into a deep sleep and woke to Robert at my bedside. "You wanna go get a bite to eat?" "Yeah, gimme a sec". "Cool, I'll be in the living room". I got dressed and walked into the large living room where several dudes were sitting, talking with Robert. The drug talk often hovered over who had the more hardcore story: a kind of retelling of their addiction days that didn't dare to glorify it, but at the same time showed how bad it was, how good they had it, and what kind of cred it gave them. Robert stood up and walked out with me to his Jag. We drove down the way to a nice Mexican place. Robert and I had been there before when I met with him just before leaving LA and Betty. We talked about all that had occurred and what the plan was. "You think Hank is gonna give us any trouble tomorrow when we go get your shit?" "I don't think so. I finally got a hold of Tahoe, he's getting back in tonight and it sounds like Hank is pretty ashamed of his behavior. He says he doesn't remember any of the time we spent together". "Yeah, that's the problem I have with a lot of addicts; it's one thing to have an addiction, but when you incorporate mental health issues with that, it's a recipe for murder, suicide, all kinds of really horrible stuff. You think he's gonna stop now?" "I don't know, but I know he has been clean and sober for long periods of time. I think it's a matter of occupying his genius mind, finding something for it to do, or shutting it up. Beer is cheap, so the demon wins. But now Tahoe is back and is horrified about it. He sent me a long email about it". "Jesus, dude. Well, I got your stuff from Betty, so you can check it out when I take you back to your room. Are you okay there?" "Yeah! Thank you so much". "This place has amazing burritos, what do you think you want?" "I'll go for the burrito the way you recommend it". "Cool".

We wrapped up the meal and Robert took me back to the house. I brought in the mail and papers from Betty to look over before bed. Robert and I agreed to meet up at nine A M. the next day to get my shit from Hank and Tahoe and then grab the Gnostic Rocket from Albert and Macy so I could clean it up to sell. That was the plan until I opened up the contract for the bike. It turns out bikes purchased the way I did cannot be sold, only the payments could be taken over. It was a blow to me because this was the saving grace that would buy me time and money and now it was gone. My only choice was to return to Washington with my tail between my legs and hope I could muster the cash to do so, because there was nothing for me in LA. I had no long term place to stay and didn't want to wear out my favors. I spoke with my family and they agreed to send me some cash to get back to Washington State. It seemed that fate wanted me there and not in LA, so I did my best to get some wind back in my sails again and plan my trip up.

I told Shawn on video chat about my change of plans and the dire trip that was to come, freely showing my embarrassment. She answered my plans with a strip tease. "You poor baby, you wanna see this?" "Oh god yes". "I wish you were here baby, I'd take care of you". Shawn had begun to writhe and squirm with her hands below my camera view. It was clear she was touching herself. Shawn was like my very own Apache angel; Native American, smooth, tan skin, full soft lips, and eyes you could fall into if you weren't careful. She begged me to talk dirty to her and it was a welcome distraction from this outright failure, so I did. I watched this feline specter as she breathed and panted and shouted and came before me and I was enthralled. "Oh my god, I've never done that before on a camera for anyone!" "I don't mind at all!" Shawn said she had to go to sleep and it made sense. She was on East Coast time and I was West, but at that moment she and I were closest.

Tears Like Flowing Streams

Nine AM came quickly and we made it to Santee Court and up to the condo. I walked in and there stood Hank, quiet and chided. He just shook his head slowly, "I'm sorry brother". Tahoe stood beside Hank silently. The occasion was like observing a funeral. I wasn't in the mood to talk, so I grabbed my shit and got out. Hank and Tahoe were supposed to be my benefactors, but there was no chance I would put myself in harm's way, to be a potential victim of the mindless whim of Hank's shadow, so now my only chance was to go back to the safe harbor of the family estate. As I came down, Robert opened the trunk of the Jag and helped me drop my stuff inside. We got on the freeway to Albert and Macy, down to Pasedena and the hills just south of the city. Robert had to hurry back, so he just let me out. I walked in to Albert and Macy and they hugged me, having received message of the Hank ordeal. "We're glad you're okay man! Jesus". I thanked Albert and Macy for letting me store the R6 there and went to uncover her. There she was, the R6, the Gnostic Rocket; my salvation on two wheels. She was my ticket to the great North West. I hit the ignition and she came to life without hesitation. It had been a while, so I let her warm up. Last time I rode her, I had come down from the icy northern hills of Humboldt and I would have to take her there once more.

I took her down the freeway and brought her up to speed, the electrifying sweetness of her precision was all the intoxication I needed. It seemed like I made it back to the sober house before I could blink. I pulled up and walked in, helmet in hand, feeling like I just stepped out of a fighter plane.

I had a day's worth of loose ends to tie up around the city, so I resolved to leave the day after next. I had too many belongings and two shelves worth of books were not going to fit on my bike with my typewriter and my backpack, so I had to give them away or sell them. The next morning I took the books to a local used bookstore. They didn't want a single one. So I made my way down to see my pal, Dave, who lived in Venice. Dave was the one who had set me up with Suze in the bay area when my exodus first began and I knew he was someone I could trust. I walked to the door, unannounced. "You want some books Dave?" Dave walked to the door with a calm, brown-bearded smile and opened the door. "What do you got for me?" "Let's see here, I've got Disinfo's *Book of Lies*, *Liber Null*, *Prometheus Rising*, *Psychedelic Shamanism*, *The Gnostic Gospels*, *Food of the Gods*, *Archaic Revival*, and a few other goodies". "Woah, those all sound pretty good!" "Oh yeah, these books can change your life. I can't take these with me, so I'd just like to give them to you". "Really? Thanks, man!" "Well, I gotta run some other errands, so I'll see you next time I'm in LA". "Well have a safe trip back to Washington, man! You'll be in my thoughts". I rode off, wrapped up the other loose ends and plotted my course to Washington the next day.

Tears Like Flowing Streams

I talked to Shawn again, "Baby, I hope you're going to be safe. It's the middle of winter. How are you going to get there without crashing?" "I'm taking the 101 up until I hit Washington. The weather looks shitty, but it's rain, not snow. 1-5 is snowed over in the mountains and there's no way I could take the bike there, so 101 is the only choice". "Gosh, that sounds so scary. Well promise me you'll be careful". "Yeah, baby, I don't want to die. It'll be okay". I plotted the course and checked the weather. Rain from Garberville to Seattle. I had a warm jacket and all of my gear from my time in Humboldt, so I knew I would be able to at least limp my way there. Morning came and I said my goodbyes to Robert and got a move on. My plan was to make it to San Francisco by dark, where this guy Adam, who I knew from social media, had offered to put me up. But this was not an easy ride. The R6 was still a sport bike and I was still fully loaded with gear. This meant the same leg pain, the same numbness, and the same lonely hours of high-speed monotony; but I had a head full of rock and roll tunes piped into my helmet and nothing to lose but my life, so off I went.

Chapter 25

I MADE IT TO SAN FRANCISCO WITH RELATIVE ease, getting some serious speed and rolling into Berkeley around seven PM. I had to pry myself off the bike when I got to the house and Adam greeted me at the door. Adam was a frail looking guy with wispy brown hair and a calm demeanor. Everything he said was seasoned with education and a psychedelic tint. The house was occupied by a broad selection of people; mostly hippie women. Adam pointed to a king size pink beanbag in the living room, "Here's where you can sleep tonight. I'm in the middle of making almond milk, you want a glass of wine, or something?" "No thanks, I need to be hangover free for this trip. I'm kind of scared. Thank you so much for putting me up". "Oh, yeah, it's no problem. I really like your work and thought it would be fun to meet you". A woman walked into the room with a long, swishy mandala-patterned dress, a topaz medallion hung around her neck. "Hi I'm Megan. Adam told me you're a writer. I looked up your stuff, super cool, man". She had a soft and wavy, close-to-stoned demeanor about her and it was very alluring. "Thanks, this house is really cool, I'm glad I decided to take Adam up on his offer for a place to crash for the night". Megan walked over to Adam, "Ruby's going to be home soon. She just messaged me. She wanted to know if we needed anything from the co-op". "No, I think we have what we need for now". "Okay, I'll let her know". I walked into the living room and dug into my bag beside the huge pink beanbag that would be my bed and found the charger for my out-of-service phone and plugged it into the wall.

The door opened up and this woman walked in wearing a sequined skirt, red shoes, red lipstick, and red hair like the secretary in *Ghostbusters*. "Hi, I'm Ruby Tuesday! I hear you've been on the road. Well you can relax here, you're welcome here as long as you like". "Thank you, Ruby, I'll be on my way in the morning, but it's nice to be somewhere that there's real people instead of some hotel". "For sure! You know, I write as well, would you like to hear some of my erotic poetry?" She stood there like a grown up Pippy Longstockings waiting for my response. "Yeah, that'd be great". Adam and Megan had heard Ruby come in and announce she'd be reading some poetry, so they all came into the living room. By this time I reposed on the pink beanbag and Megan dropped down beside me, close enough to be intimate, but not so close to impose any activity of amorous nature.

Tears Like Flowing Streams

Ruby stood before us with her notebook and qualified her poem. "So, I am polyamorous and love sex. I have multiple orgasms per intercourse session and am very aware of this temple that is my body. I describe these things in ways that defy shame and ignorance to sex".

Ruby stood there with a slight kink in her hip, ready to move as she spoke, all eyes attended.

Slowly hands flow like streams of water
Slowly I sway like somber tides
The fingers rush over the falls of my love
And into the sacred place they enter
Steady and firm they move in rhythm and grace
Legs slide against one another
like a fiddle and bow

Ruby touched below her stomach, just to the side of her center, curling fingers like a Balinese dancer:

And up it comes like water from a well
Out it flows to cure the drought

She stood rigid as a steel beam with one hand in the air: "YES, YES, YESSSSSSS!"

Megan's head was pressed close to mine, the smell of incense permeated her black, curly locks. We cheered Ruby's poetry and settled in for the night. I slept alone on the beanbag, charged with all the sexual energy the room had been filled with, but I was too exhausted to try my way into either Ruby or Megan's beds, so I slept. In the morning,

I ate a nutrition bar I had bought the day before and packed up my things. Megan emerged from her room and gave me a stone. "This will give you good fortune. It is filled with my care and power, it won't fail you". I thanked Megan and popped my head into Adam's room and thanked him for having me over, packed up and hit the road again.

The weather had been better than expected and so far not a drop of rain had fallen on me. This made the crisp winter air bearable. Once again I crossed the bridge on the 101 from the Bay Area and once again I was taken by the beauty of it all in the morning fog. I knew where I was going, so I just hunkered down for another day of aching away on the bike. My final destination was the town of Arcata, the place where all of this wildness had really begun. The day was long and cold, with the wind whipping through any space between my helmet and jacket as I cruised up the 101. When I finally made it to Arcata, I checked in at a hostel and cleaned myself up in the showers. I didn't want to be alone, so I went to the bar down the street, in that same town square that I had first met Baby Jesus and Ben and all the others. This time, I was just passing through and not looking for work, but I was looking for girls. I had a couple of drinks, looked around, but nobody was interesting, or interested, so I went back to the hostel and slept.

After checking out and gassing up, I cruised along the 101 past the park I illegally slept in and

Tears Like Flowing Streams

on into unknown territory. I had never been this far north on the 101 and found out pretty quickly that it is a long stretch of road. Before I knew it, it was dusk and the air got colder and colder. Being two-thirds of the way through February and riding in tandem to the ocean, there was no shelter from the constant buffeting of winter's touch. After six hours of riding, I still hadn't seen the Oregon border. The roads twisted more and more, and the speed limit got slower and slower. I began to feel numb and sleepy from the monotony of the ride and followed the car in front of me in a dangerous headspace. My eyes began to blur and the movements seemed delayed, but on the other hand, I felt like I was tractor-beamed to the car in front of me.

The roads swayed up and down like a rollercoaster and went on and on, as if they were mercilessly doing all of this to me on purpose. After an agonizingly long time, I came upon a town. I pulled in at a gas station and talked up the clerk. "Are there any good hotels around here for a weary traveler? You know the rates by any chance? I was hoping to get to Coos Bay tonight". "Oh, well Coos Bay is another two hours from here. The hotels here are around $120 per night". "Oh shit, I can't do that. I just need a hole to hide in till dawn. I'll have fifteen dollars on pump two, this coffee, and these gloves". "That'll be nineteen dollars fifty-three. Well if you keep going, you'll need to look out for elk. They are everywhere and cars hit them every day along the road between here and

Coos Bay. I'd be extremely careful on that bike". I waved thanks to the attendant and pumped the gas and drank my coffee. She told me there was a Motel 6 in Coos Bay and that it would probably be the cheapest.

I put the new cloth gloves on and slid my motorcycle gloves over them so I could keep my hands warm. The cold had become bitter, but it also acted as an agent to fight my lethargy. As I cruised along the highway, I kept a watchful eye for elk and luckily, didn't see a single one. The time went agonizingly slow though, because I was cold, exhausted, and emotionally rough, but I finally made it to the motel and got a room. The décor was a strange kind of badly done modernism, where bright orange and lime green were liberally used. There was wifi, so I talked to Shawn for a while on video, describing the day's journey and telling her how much I thought about her along the way. "Well, I'm glad I'm helping to keep you alive mister. I can't make love to you one day if you're gonna go and die". We said goodnight and I cranked the heat in the room and slept in my fleece blanket under the hotel bed covers. There are some kinds of cold that take extreme swaddling to combat, and I had been in that kind of cold all day and night.

I awoke in the morning and ate the "continental breakfast" which consisted of a bagel with cream cheese, a Danish, a banana, and coffee. I guess it counted since bagels are Jewish, Danishes

Tears Like Flowing Streams

are Danish, and bananas and coffee are from South America. While I filled up for gas, a girl on a pink scooter saluted me like motorcyclists on the highway do, a left hand held down to the side. I thought this may have been the most adorable thing I had seen in some time. The folks who live outside of the big cities have a manner that you can see and feel without even talking and this was one such way. I rode the R6 inland through southern Oregon, having routed the mountains and needing to get back on I-5. As I made my way through the small towns and two-lane highways, I came across a lush field where a large herd of elk had come to graze. These were a threat to my life on the midnight ride, but here they were my boon and inspiration. Smitten by the natural beauty of my surroundings I was full of love for nature herself, devoid of the myopia that we highfalutin primates had so often brandished, the trees and plants of the forest and all of its animals exemplified the simple, subtle elegance of being.

I finally made it onto I-5 and brought the rocket up to speed. It had been two days since I could keep her at seventy miles-per-hour at length, so I reveled in the pace of progress and looked forward to seeing another internet friend, King Louis, who had invited me to stay with him and his girlfriend Gypsy in Portland. I made it there before dark and pulled up to his house. Though we had never met before, we had shared a lot of mutual interests and got to talking immediately. We went out for pho and discussed life, the journey, and the power of psychedelics. On the way back, we picked up some beers and got good and tanked, describing our views on the legalization of weed in Washington State, the details of present psychedelic research, and the greatness and challenges of love. I passed out on the couch and got myself ready for the last two hours of riding that would return me to the family home out on the peninsula. After days of misery and pain on the road, two hours seemed like nothing at all. So I said goodbye to King Louis and Gypsy, whom I had only met as I walked out the door and made my way home. When I pulled into the driveway after all of that work, I felt a sigh of relief and a chill of fear; fear that I wouldn't be able to pull something together; fear that I wouldn't get into school for lack of good credit, or good grades; fear that I would never have a home of my own, or a stable situation. The golem in my mind had never been far and was once again whispering words of failure in my ear.

I was welcomed by my step-mother and my father and found rest and solace. I finalized the details of my third book, published it, and did my best to focus on the good things going on. I was now in Washington as a resident, and it was good to see my kids more. I spent my days building fences with my brother, Jim, and writing promotional articles for the book on ecstatic states. Shawn and I spoke for hours in the evenings. We had grown emotionally close even though we had never seen each other. There was, of course the emotional challenge of a long distance relationship, but I had no doubt she was stunning, and she seemed emotionally stable. Things with the book began to take off, at least in my little niche of the psychedelic world, and people began to take notice of what I was writing. But the seeming string of defeats in planning left me wondering if a return to the corporate war machine was still a viable option. I fought against my ethical concerns and submitted my résumé for my old position, which was hiring. In the meantime I had book sales and construction to live on. I thought maybe work could pay for school and I could do them both, having nobody else to answer to as far as where my money was spent. I tried to just let the idea go and see what would come of it, but it lingered in my mind. I was torn because the peninsula was safe, but it was lonely. Safety was good and I was about as low as a person could get in money, love, and tangible success. At least this was the way I felt. Shawn, distant and goddess-like, stood in the distance, her breasts heaving and her giant brown eyes glistening with welcome. She became my goal and motivation, the prize for doing things the way the world wanted me to.

As things progressed with Shawn, I fell head over heels in love with her and she reflected the same emotions. She was everything I wanted; pretty, earth friendly, tattooed and world-wise; floppy sun hats and long paisley dresses, folk songs and psychedelics, whisky and perversion. She was an Apache princess, whose stature and curves made me weak of will and I was fully under the spell.

"I want to come and see you in June, would that be okay?" "June? Yeah, that would be great, but maybe I could come see you sooner and then you could come see me?" "Yeah, that would be wonderful! I can't stand being this far away from you and not seeing you baby, you've totally stolen my heart!" "I feel the same way, little lady". As time and chance would have it, my brother James was going through a divorce and had been in Washington, in the same kind of spirit that I was; we had both been called back to the place of our birth.

Chapter 26

JAMES NEEDED TO GO TO MINNESOTA IN March to pick up his belongings from his wife, Catherine, and he asked me to come along. We had reunited over the last while and commiserated over our similar lovelorn situations. He, too, had come to an impasse, where his spiritual resurgence and harrowing desire to live life outside of popular constraints drove him to the edge of madness, depression, and anxiety. He too had to change and we recognized that we had been running along parallel paths.

James was a good nine years older than me, and as my big brother could be a total dick at times, but life had worn down his hard edges, and what therapy and self-study didn't chip away, the Ayahuasca did. We were now on a close, but not even footing. The balance of power still was uneven and we were unsure who was the teacher, or the pupil, between us.

I agreed to take the trip to Minnesota with him and saw this as an opportunity to go see Shawn in South Carolina. I talked to her about it and she was thrilled at the news, "If you come here, I may keep you hostage as my love slave. You can stay as long as you want!" My book sales had taken off and I now had five hundred dollars. This was enough to buy the ticket and cover a couple of bills while I was away, so I went for it. I was set on making progress, settling in after I made my way back from this trip. James picked me up and we headed down the highway over the mountains and into eastern Washington. The landscape changed from wet, green vistas to tan, tall grass, and farmland. After a couple of hours we made it to Idaho and watched the sun go down as we rode the concrete wave across the land. The tone of our trip was both adventurous and somber as we used the time mostly to discuss matters of the heart.

James used to be a police officer, and despite his similarities to me he had a sterner overtone, at least with me. Where I was always wearing my thoughts on my sleeve, his every phrase was calculated, protected by layers of security, and equipped with an out. In our adult relationship, I was always the one to have a fucked up and stupid explanation for something I had done. I was always the one who needed to be guided and directed. But we bonded on our simple need to be loved and understood, and that was the foundation we had established in the months leading up to this trip. We were to stay at a friend's cabin in Montana, and we agreed to take turns driving until we made it there. James played Tom Petty, "It's time to move on, it's time to get goin'", and it felt right to hear the sounds of a simple man making big changes, not with the vulgarity of the dim-witted and cruel, but by making the best of where we really were. We were two broken men trying to make sense of something so good and elusive that we could hardly articulate what was going on.

I had it all figured out, though, I was going to give in to corporate sensibility and get a high powered job for that big jet company and make a shitton of money, then I was going to use that cash to pay for school and eliminate my debts, then I was going to buy a little piece of property for me and Shawn and we would make a little homestead and I would teach in a nearby town's community college. James balked at the idea, citing the three thousand miles of separation between her and I, the fact that she was stunningly beautiful and might not want to wait for a broke writer to get his shit together, and lastly, the fact that we both had so much we wanted to do individually that it might not be enough.

I ignored this, because she was pretty, because she said she loved me, because I wanted to taste her and touch her and find that home I had been looking for in her. What could be so wrong with going to see a girl that you'd built a couple of months talking to, getting to know and sharing dreams with? I had no reason to doubt it, but James still had reservations about the situation, ill at ease with my choice to see a girl so far from my barely established home.

We made it to the cabin around two AM after spending half an hour driving up and down dirt roads looking for it. The tall trees obscured any views from the road, so we relied on James's memory of the roads to get us there. The security lights came on as we pulled up and got out. It was ultra quiet, majestic, and spooky. We grabbed our bags and got in; James flipped on the lights. "Let's see if they got any booooze!" he said as he curled his fingers, hands in the air, employing his playful voice. "Ah, shit man, all they got is this vanilla-cherry-infused vodka. You want a pull?" "Sure". He poured some vodka into a glass and I took a drink; it tasted awful, like cough syrup and rubbing alcohol. I grabbed a beer from the fridge to wash out the ghastly afterglow of fake vanilla and cherry. James took a drink too and opted for a beer instead. I finished his. I wanted to drink more, maybe stay up for an hour or so to get a good buzz, but James suggested we get to sleep after the one beer. I agreed, since there wasn't anything good to drink anyway. James took the room upstairs while I settled into the guest room downstairs. The bed was covered in dog fur but I was really tired and didn't really have a choice of where to sleep. Morning came quickly.

I awoke to the sound and smells of breakfast. "Lil' brudder, getcho ass up! We're leaving in twenty minutes!" I groggily crawled out of the bed

Tears Like Flowing Streams

and wandered into the kitchen. James had found some bacon and pastries, so we made quick work of them. We cleaned up our mess and headed out to his truck, planning to stop in the Badlands. Up to this point, I hadn't really known much about the Badlands, so I was interested in seeing them. "It's like landing on the moon", James said with a big smile and wiggling eyebrows. "A very spiritual place. It blows my mind every time I visit. You're going to love it". James popped in the Beastie Boys' *Ill Communication* album and we started down the road once again. People close to me know that I am a frequent talker and it's rarely something about basic stuff. I'm always rattling on about consciousness, religion, psychedelics, occultism, and the arguments between scientists about whether we will ever be able to measure what happens in the realm of mind and whether it's entirely within our mind, or if we reach out. After James has had enough of this conversation, he just picks a CD and plays it, so I'll get the hint and shut the fuck up.

As the day dragged on we continued to talk about how he was feeling, what he had gone through, the painful questions one must ask when they are ending a marriage. There were moments where his levity sunk instantaneously to tears, where my big brother's voice trembled as he spoke. Before that trip, I had only seen him cry once and it was for the same reason that I began to cry with him.

We called ahead to the Badlands State Park and reserved a cabin. As we rolled through the hills and valleys, America opened up to me. It's a beautiful place and it baffles me when people say we don't have enough space to make food, or there isn't enough room for housing. Anyone who has driven across this nation has seen how much unused space there is. That is not to say we should turn the whole thing into a big city, but that we are being robbed and lied to when they say "there isn't enough".

Night fell as we drove and James put in U2's *Achtung Baby*. The mood for the drive followed every dynamic high and low of that album; every song sung to us like it was written just for that moment. We were living the words and the bad feelings felt good. We were getting close and James reminded me that this was a solemn and mystical place, full of strange history and a magical air, so I tried my best to prepare myself for something good. As we made our way past the state park entrance, the first white peaks ghosted by in the headlights, the road was beset on all sides by sedimentary rock formations that looked extra strange in the dead of night. James stopped the truck and we walked up one of the hills and stared up at the sky, U2 still rattling and humming from the truck. And just like he said, it was like traversing the surface of the moon. In the night, the cold air and light breeze seemed to lift us up right into the sky itself, showing us the bare and miniscule nature of our existence. We were so small under that big sky.

After getting the key to the cabin we made our way in. It was a fourteen-by-twenty-four single room with a bathroom in the back and no kitchen. The log cabin was equipped with two beds, wifi, and a fresh set of towels for the shower. It was all that we needed for the night. With only two days left before seeing Shawn, I was beside myself with excitement. I dreamed of seeing her, holding her, making love to her, and starting a new chapter in my life; one where I didn't compromise my values because I hadn't learned to love myself enough. I called her through a wifi phone line and let her know I was safe. "I'm so excited to see you! I can't believe you're going to be here so soon! I've made everything ready, so all you have to do is get here". "I can't wait to see you either, baby". "Well, call me from the road and let me know how it's going". "Will do". We turned off the lights and got to sleep.

When I woke in the morning, James was already up, just laying there. He heard me stir and muttered with a slow, sedate tone. "You up brother?" "Yeah". "Let's go get some breakfast and take a walk". I checked my phone and saw a message from Shawn. "We need to talk, I don't know if you coming is such a good idea". I looked at that message and my heart slung into my stomach. What the fuck did she mean by "we need to talk?" That must be the worst phrase in the English language. I wrote her back asking to call me and she did. "I just got this promotion at the bar and I'll be managing things there. It's a lot of responsibility and will be really good experience for me, but it's going to take a lot of time and effort. I don't know if I'll even be able to hang out with you while you're here, except when I'm off. Is there, like any way you can change your flight to come in a month or so?" "What? No, I can't change the ticket, I'm flying out to you tomorrow. Baby, I don't care if you work fourteen-hour days, I just want to see you, to be with you, even if it's just us sleeping in the same bed. We've been talking for months now and I want to see you. Don't you want to see me?" "Well, yeah, but I don't know if I can. Is there, like anywhere you can stay once you get off the plane, maybe for a couple of days? I mean you can't just hang out at my bar while I'm working. That would be unprofessional". "No, I don't know anyone in South Carolina. Listen, if I don't fly out, I'll just have to cancel and I don't know if I'll be able to come again any time soon. Just let me come see you. I really want to see you and I know you want to see me too". "Oh gosh, okay. I'm sorry, I'm just freaked out. I want to be perfect for you and I feel like you're just going to be sitting around and I'm gonna look like shit". "So you were gonna leave me at the airport?! C'mon, we've been talking for months, everything is going to be okay". "Ok baby, I'm sorry. I just freaked out. Come see me, I want to see you so bad. Come see me". "Okay, I will".

Tears Like Flowing Streams

James saw I was obviously upset. "What was that all about?" "Shawn got freaked out that she wasn't going to be able to spend any time with me while I was there and she wanted me to reschedule". "What? That's weird. Is she okay?" "Yeah, she just got nervous, I guess". "Shit, have you seen yourself? Your ass is janky as fuck. I don't blame her". "Thanks for that".

We packed up the truck so we wouldn't have to do anything after the walk but leave. We grabbed our food from the free breakfast-to-go and walked as we ate. James had a somber look on his face, like he was chewing on his own broken heart, and I tried to encourage him. "Listen, I'm here with you, I came so you would know you weren't alone. You're my big brother, I love you. We're gonna get through all this trouble, because we know we're gonna see that happy day when we finally achieve what we've waited for, that happy life where we are whole alone, but don't have to be, because we've found the one we love". "I can't think about that shit right now". We walked together for a while among the spired pyramids of the Badlands and parted ways for a bit. I climbed up to the top of a large spire, stood for a while and walked back down. The hill was steep and the rock was slippery, so in my flat-footed boots I slid a couple feet down on my ass, making a big scrape down my side. James ran over to me to make sure I was okay and we took my spill as the cue to go. As we drove away, James quipped: "We need to bring our sons here for a rite of passage. We never had anything like that and we should establish something for them, an acknowledgment of their changing position in our families. We should honor them as they grow. We should do something for Gwyneth too, when it's time". "Yeah, that sounds like a good thing to do, try to show them through ritual the changes that they are going through, show them the turning point from childhood to adulthood. I dig it".

Today was the day we would make it to our destination, when James would see Catherine again after many months of separation. It loomed over the morning. As we started to drive, I picked up the banter and James pulled to the side of the road without a word. He pulled a piece of paper from a notepad in his center console. I sat there and watched as he drew two little boxes on the pad. Above the boxes read:

James' mood today:
Sacred / Profane

James checked the "Sacred" box and handed me the paper. I got the hint. I took this to heart, knowing that there was a fine line between keeping things light and annoying the shit out of somebody who was wrestling with internal dialogue. I pulled my sweatshirt over my head and took a nap. When I awoke we were just about to reach the Minnesota border and the scenery seemed to change overnight. Everything looked like...well, Minne-

Tears Like Flowing Streams

sota. We made it to his old house after an hour or so and we were both somber. Catherine came out to greet us, "Hey guys, glad to see you made it safe". James walked in with her alone while I sat in the truck. After all that time in there, I didn't mind staying just a bit longer. James emerged from the garage and waved for me to come in. The house was immaculately taken care of, the décor was flawless, the pantries were full of healthy, but delicious foods, and there was booze to spare. After so much transient living in random houses, on floors, in the studio apartments of girls, and on the side of the road, this place was like heaven.

Catherine and James had done something I was not familiar with; they were getting a divorce like adults: measured steps, individual counseling, vision quests, considerations, trial separation, and finally, what we had now, the dissolution. Catherine was well lettered, regal, demure, well kept, and totally crushed by all of this. It was written on her face and it filled the place with a warm and full kind of sadness I had never felt; a justified, even dignified sadness. It was as if the tears shed in that house were noble and the splitting of these two was tragic, but pure. It was a hard thing to be around. Catherine showed me to the guest room and I put my things down, preparing for my flight to South Carolina in the morning. James' son, Cam, volunteered to take me there at five AM. I settled in for the night and woke at 4:30, gathered my things, and waited for Cam. I had about 160 dollars to my name by this time and it had to last me one week, so I kept the airport food to a minimum.

I made it through security and got on the plane to Charlotte, where I would have a four-hour layover before flying into Spartanburg, to the loving arms of my sweet southern belle. I got hungry during the layover and ended up buying some nasty fast food. I spent my time trying to find a comfortable way to nap, but there never is anywhere to nap in an airport, so I ended up just being really tired. Even in the airport, I could feel the southern air, a scent not unfamiliar to me since I had lived what seemed a lifetime ago in Nashville. The feeling is wet, sticky, sweet, and pervasive; there is simply nowhere to go to hide from it.

Chapter 27

THE SOUTH GETS INTO YOUR BONES ONCE YOU are there, like the thickness of pancakes with syrup, or the grease from thick-cut bacon; it seeps in and you can't help but soak it up like a sponge. I boarded the regional prop-plane to Spartanburg and prepared myself for meeting Shawn, the ravenhaired, golden-voiced, doe-eyed, smoldering vixen of love that I had fallen for through the internet. As the plane rushed over the lush greenery of South Carolina, I was stricken with two parts excitement and one part shock. This was her, this was it, I was going to see my rock and roll queen. We disembarked and I walked through the little airport and down to the baggage claim where the exits were. I was really nervous and wanted to ensure I didn't stink, so I took off my socks and changed into some clean ones. I fixed my hair in the bathroom mirror and walked out into the midday sun. At first, I didn't see her and decided to just stand there for a bit and collect my thoughts, then I saw her face, bright and beautiful, wreathed in tendrils of black, eyes brown as chocolate. I walked up to the car and we both made awkward movements, but I leaned in for a hug and a kiss. Without any hesitation I got in the car and we drove off.

I had never been in an official relationship with someone whose body I had never touched. I didn't know what to do. The shock value took over my internal equation. I asked her if it was okay to touch her hair, to lean my head on her, and she said yes. "I'm so sorry, but I have to drop you off at my place and go straight to work, but I'll come straight home to you, okay?" "Sure, sweetheart, whatever you need. I don't require anything. I'm just here to see you". "Okay". We drove along the highway, which faced constant threat of encroachment by the surrounding vegetation of the South and headed down along the side of a lake and onto a small road that led to her house. "This is the place. It isn't fancy, but it's home for now". The house was a little blue rambler set on a small hillside, a large willow tree wept over the crabgrass lawn that was so coarse you wouldn't want to walk on it with bare feet. I followed Shawn into her room; a studio apartment, connected by a door to the rest of the house, where she introduced me to Angie and her soon to be ex-husband, Chris.

"It's nice to meet you, Shawn has told me so much about you!" Angie said in her adorable southern accent. "It's lies! All Lies!" I jokingly cried, waving my hands like Richard Nixon. "Thank you for letting me stay at your home. I promise not to

Tears Like Flowing Streams

be a burden. I'm low maintenance, I'll probably spend most of my time in Shawn's room writing and preparing for some interviews I have coming up". "Well, you don't have to stay in there, please feel free to come watch TV, or play video games". Just then two little faces peered from outside a doorway down the hall. One little girl, about five years old, and the other, just a toddler. I waved at the children and tried to not look like a big scary man, but who knows how a giant of a man looks with a gaping smile. I waved hello with a gentle gesture. "It's okay girls, you can come out. This is Shawn's friend. He's gonna be at the house for a while".

The two scurried out, the older leading the way, the toddler wearing nothing but a diaper and walking clumsily with a finger in her ear. "I'm Sadie! Can I touch your beard? Why's it white? Are you an old man?" I leaned down to Sadie and let her touch my beard, the toddler followed suit and touched my face. "The little one is Amber", Angie quipped. Amber looked up at her mom, forgetting she was touching my face. I looked to Sadie and said, "Well, I don't know what happened, Sadie, I've had this white beard since I was in my mid-twenties and I figured since I had it, I shouldn't be afraid to show it". "I like it, you look like a wizard! Are you a wizard?" "Actually, I am a wizard, but I only use my powers for good and never evil". "That's good! Bye!" Sadie and Amber thumped their way back into the other room as fast as they came and I smiled, lightened by their presence. Shawn looked at her phone, "Oh gosh, I gotta go! There's food in the fridge and this is my cupboard, so eat whatever you want. I'll be home around two AM so you'll have to wait to see me, mister!" "Sounds good, love. Have a great night at work". Shawn rushed out the door and drove away. I settled into her room and organized my things in a non-invasive manner.

Shawn had a kitten she had named Baba, which was an alright name, but he had a black and white face, painted like a black metal band member, so I renamed him "Murderface". He would run up and scratch me, bite my hand and try to kill me at all times, as is the custom of kittens. I took a nap and would wake from time to time to the sound of screaming children and yelling parents. Angie, though sweet and kind, was fairly hands off with her kids and would intervene only once a kid was crying, or the wall had been drawn on.

Later on in the evening, Chris came home and introduced himself to me. He seemed like a well-meaning, but hopelessly oblivious guy, and I felt a great deal of compassion for him and his situation. Whenever he wasn't around, Angie would talk shit about what a "pussy" he was, but would revert to a kind of morose form of love and talk about how sweet he was to the girls. It was strange, being a total stranger in a house where divorce was occurring. It made me think of Betty, it made me think of James and Catherine, it made me think of the

Tears Like Flowing Streams

mother of my children; more so it made me ponder the ways of love and how we are all fighting for its truth, but can never seem to find that truth for ourselves, only a grasping at shadows, pawing at a laser like Murderface; never quite catching what we thought we had for sure.

I awoke around 1:45, excited for Shawn to arrive, so I went and brushed my teeth and combed my hair. Her Saab pulled into the driveway and she burst in the door with a bottle of Jameson. "You want some whiskey, baby?" She ran into the kitchen and got two glasses and filled them with ice, "Work went so long knowing you were here in my bed! I just wanted to run straight home and jump on you". She let her hair down and took her shoes off and poured the two glasses to the top with whiskey, handing me one. She looked at me with her ravenous eyes and sipped her whiskey, then with it still unswallowed, let it out of her mouth into mine and I drank it. We kissed and the drinks were quickly set aside, our clothes came quickly off, and we were making love. She scratched on my back and pulled at me hard as I moved inside her. "I want you to tie me to the posts! Tie me to the posts!" This distracted me more than turned me on. "Grab those silk scarves". I tied her down and made my way back inside her. "Oh, oh! Baby I've wanted you for so long! Oh my gosh!" It didn't take long before we had both come to climax and I let her loose. I looked down, still over her tan and well-figured body, her eyes looking up at me like the Whore of Babylon as she slid her fingers inside herself and brought them to her mouth. "Mmmm, you taste so good" She said like she had been reading a script. We laid next to each other and drank our whiskey until the glasses were empty, just holding hands and touching, writhing, and kissing. I had been in her physical presence for less than two hours, but we had talked for months and I had never burned so hot for someone. We talked about our plans to live in the countryside and I told her that I would be sure to get this big paying job at the jumbo jet company and pay for my schooling with it. I would be a professor, and we would live a simple life and I would take care of her. "That sounds amazing, baby! There's nothing I want more than to be with you". We talked until four in the morning and fell asleep with a good buzz.

At seven AM the screaming of children and parents ensued and it was hard to fall back asleep. Amber and Sadie would burst into the room while we were asleep and Angie would have to coax them out. I got up and locked the door. Shawn slept right through it and snored like a tiny motorboat. I got up to pee and waved at the tiny faces in the hall before going back. "Are you awake yet? We wanna see Shawn! Is Shawn awake?!" I whispered back: "No, she got home late from work". "My mom works with Shawn, that's why she sleeps on the couch!" "Ohhhh, I see". I made the be quiet sign to the girls and Sadie loudly whispered, "Okayyy!"

Tears Like Flowing Streams

I curled up around Shawn while Murderface attacked my butt. I tried to ignore him as he needled me through and through. Shawn woke up and looked up at me. "It's like I'm dreaming, you're actually here". She rubbed her eyes and stretched her tattooed arms out around my neck. "How could I ever go to work, when I know you're here?" "I don't know baby, I'm just happy I'm here with you now. We got up and She made me breakfast and Sadie clung to my leg, hugging it like a monkey "I like you! Can I be your girlfriend?" "No, honey, I'm Shawn's boyfriend. I'm sorry!" Shawn looked with laughing eyes at me as she made a salad and an ornate arrangement of tomatoes and avocado. A single egg, fried beside the spread, elegantly plated. "Here you are, handsome!"

I sat down and ate, enjoying that it was made just for me and enjoying that it was made well. It felt like love. Shawn had to run some errands for work, so I came along for the ride and we saw the local town. The place was full of well-built houses for the most part, with the exception of the occasional single-wide trailer. The people seemed genuinely friendly and everyone of course spoke with a thick southern drawl. Shawn grabbed what she needed and we made it back to the house in time for me to be dropped off. "Oh, man, I need to go to work again. I'll see you tonight when I get home. Message me if you want and I'll check it as the night goes on". "Okay, sweetheart". After she drove off, I thought I'd take a walk and explore, so I put on my boots, my blue jeans, and my Motörhead t-shirt and walked down into the deep, murky green of unknown.

As I meandered, cardinals wisped like red kites between the trees, just fast enough to catch your eye. The southern sun slid through the leaves of the forest on both sides of the road and showed the heavy air in its beams. I kept walking and walking, since there was nothing else to do, until I made my way up and over a ridge in the road, where I could see the lake we had passed. I walked down and stood on the bank where thin, red-barked trees clung to the edge of the water, dipping their roots right into the lake. It looked like they were giant spiders frozen in place with their spindled legs creeping in to wade. I stood in the silence, marveling at the fact that I was here in South Carolina, of all places, seeing a rock and roll girl from New York who was hiding from all of its vices. Shawn admitted to having a coke problem in New York and that she drank too much there. She said she barely ever drank at all anymore except on special occasions. I too was hiding from the party in many ways, having felt like I had outgrown the scene that at one point been my deepest identifying factor. I used to be a New Yorker, a guy who knew the celebrities and bankers by name and drank good whiskey most nights. I was the guy who had a bartender friend at every good bar, got comped, got drunk. I got into the Jane Hotel's private club when the movie stars were partying there. I made money and was miserable in a marriage with a person whose idea of success was perennially raised a little higher than the success we presently had. It was never enough. Now I stood at the banks of a nameless lake wondering if I would hear from the big jet company about that fancy job offer, allowing myself to tempt fate and become the slave to all that I hated with the fickle promise that I might one day be free to be myself and make a living at it.

I walked back to the house and noticed a rifle range on the side of the road, apparently for public use. It weirded me out to think that this was normal, having a firing range out in the open, just a hundred yards or so from the nearest house. When I got back inside, I played with Murderface for a while and settled in to write some friends. I checked on James who said he might need me to change my return date to Minnesota, and that I should be prepared to do so. I checked in with Dr. August and told him how things were going and we chatted about his love life a bit. But the early wake up from the kids left me groggy, so I napped again. When I woke up there were still several hours before I would see Shawn again, so I did my best to read my books and do some write-ups for my book. I saw that I would have a check coming my way soon and celebrated this fact, since the small amount of cash I had was slowly dwindling.

I opened up my email to a message I didn't want to see:

Thank you for your interest in the Big Jet Company! We appreciate the time you took to complete our online application process for the following position: Requisition: 24-1028916; Job Title: Procurement Agent 8. Unfortunately, this job opening has been cancelled.

Chapter 28

WHEN SHAWN GOT HOME, IT WAS NEARLY three-thirty and she was visibly drunk. I had been meditating and reading all day, sitting in her room like it was my own little cabin. She was upset and had a wild look of worry in her eyes, "I didn't make any tips tonight. I...I just...I can't do this, you know...I mean who are you? Who the fuck are you? You're here in my house, my bed, and you're eating my food?" I was totally taken by surprise, having spoken with her for months and making love to her the night before, being made breakfast, and sending love messages all day. "Baby, I'm your boyfriend that came across this big ass country to come see you because we had to see each other, remember? If you want money, I can pay for food and gas. I don't need much and I'm not here to be a burden on you". "Well, you can't just stay here the whole time, you can't just show up and stay here". She teetered as she spoke, with a dull sag in her eyes. "Wait, so you want me to leave right now? I have nowhere to go! I'm in the middle of nowhere in the deep South. Baby, come here!" Shawn softened at my call and sat on the edge of the bed. I scooted over to be beside her. "I'm here because I want you. I want to be with you, be your man and you want to be my lady. I'm here to prove to you that I'm real and that I mean what I say. I love you". Shawn snapped out of her worried, drunken outburst and went to take a shower. I was shocked and scared, wondering if that was a one time thing, or if she was going to abandon me on the side of the road with no money. By this point in my travels I had pretty much worn out every favor from every friend and it was time to rely only on whatever means I had in the time and place and with something like eighty dollars in my pocket, it seemed like I didn't have all that much to work with.

Shawn was in the bathroom for about forty-five minutes and I drank whiskey as I waited for her, hoping the drunkenness I was gaining would match the drunkenness she was losing, like we'd meet someplace in the middle. When she came back, her hair was done up, she was in a grey pencil skirt and a white top, buttoned down, showing off her bulging breasts. I was full of anxiety from the outburst and she tried to console me. She stood at the edge of the bed and told me to stand up. I walked around to where she stood and she bent over and put her hands, one over the next along the footboard of the bed, with her ass waving before me in the short skirt. "I want you to spank me, baby!" I tried my best to change gears in my head from the terror of being thrown out into the dark in snake and cockroach country, to dominating master of dirty secretaries. I gave her a good single spank, to which she winced and let out a gasp. "Harder, please!" WHACK! "AH, OH GOD! AGAIN!" I brought my hand down hard on her finely curved ass as she let out a gasp and turned around, grabbing my manhood. I was limp and small.

Shawn felt around and looked at me with surprise and sadness, "What? What is it baby? What do you want? Don't you want to fuck me?" I stood there embarrassed and confused with my limp dick, gazing at this pornographic vision of love, this woman who burned a hole in my heart and soul, poised for me to take. The entire lower half of my body felt clenched like an angry fist, refusing to do anything but panic. "I can't. I just can't". "What do you mean you can't?" She put my hands on her breasts and licked her tongue at me. I want to do anything you want. You wanna put it in my butt? I've never done that before". Nothing she said turned me on. It was like I had been sent to hell for every day of my life that I masturbated to steamy scenes of slutty women and this was my punishment, to have it and not be able to take it.

"*Ugh!* This is so embarrassing! You don't want me, do you?! You don't think I'm sexy". "No, no, no, it's okay, I just…" She grabbed her bathrobe and took off her high heels and went into the bathroom once more. I took a drink of whiskey and looked at the glass, wondering if maybe drinking had finally made its way to my sex drive. I took another drink and waited for her to burst in as she had previously done.

The door swung open and her face was red with anger. "I'm going to sleep on the couch, you can stay in here". "What? What? No, baby, please let me explain!" She stopped for a moment, fuming with embarrassed rage. "This has never happened to me before. But moments ago you were going to throw me out into the street and I just found out they cancelled the job I was going for, and I'm still tired from all of this travel. Please don't sleep out there! Just stay with me here, just be with me. I totally want you, but I'm scared of you, scared you're going to change your mind about me and it makes my dick not trust you. That's all I can guess. I don't know what's going on. Just come here, please!" I tried not to seem pitiful, but my dick and I both felt about an inch tall.

Shawn crawled over to me and kissed me, her buzz now back down to a manageable level. "It's okay baby, I understand. I know you want me. I understand you're scared. I'm not gonna kick you out. I love you". She kissed me some more, but I was on the verge of tears. She took her clothes off and I took off mine and we clung to each other and fell asleep. When the sun came up, the light shone through the laced curtain and glistened in beams through the room, falling on Shawn as she slept sweet and majestic like the devil's only bride.

Tears Like Flowing Streams

I kissed her face and she quietly stirred. She rolled over to me and looked at me with innocent eyes, as if she had known nothing of the night before. I had seen this face on another in recent memory, but I didn't want to admit the same demon that plagued Hank might be inside my Apache angel.

Shawn got up and went to the bathroom. I stood up and stretched out the hangover I had. When she returned, she pulled off her bathrobe and lay down on the bed before me. She spread her legs on display to me, and what I saw was beautiful. I told her I was scared that the same thing would happen as the night before. "It's okay. Put your mouth on me". I did and spent my time enjoying what I was doing and felt the fearful bunny that was my dick returning from the safety of his hiding place. I entered her and we made love. The emotion of the night before had brought out a new kind of orgasm, one that I rarely felt, an odd mixture of shame, lust, fascination, and love. Shawn came to climax and we laid there, spent and relieved that it was a one time deal.

Chapter 29

SINCE I WAS IN THE SOUTH, I MADE PLANS TO meet with my friend Metcalfe , a reclusive authority on the much-feared Santa Muerte cult of Mexican drug lords. Metcalfe lived in near Elberton, Georgia, where the mysterious Georgia Guidestones were erected. Metcalfe was a recluse, but he lived with his long-time roommate and witchy friend, Willow. I had arranged to borrow Shawn's car while she was at work to go visit him and meet another esoteric expert at the Guidestones. The drive was about two hours and money was tight, but I had enough to do it and there was no time like the present. I dropped off Shawn, who seemed to be in a much better state of mind than the frenetic days prior, and assured her I would take good care of her Saab. I didn't have a phone, so I had to use screen shots I had established when I had wifi. When I finally got to the Guidestones, I met up with the camera crew that was going to film our talk. There was no sign of Metcalfe and word had reached us that he didn't have money for gas to get to the spot. I volunteered to go get him with some cash from the film-maker. I borrowed the dude's GPS and followed the coordinates deep into the obscure and dense backroads of rural Georgia, where I got lost more than once. I had never seen roads this bad, bumpy, and unmarked in all of my life. By some kind of magic, I found my way to his shack in the dark, dense belly of the southern woods. I hadn't seen Metcalfe since we first met in New York, when we were both writing for *Reality Sandwich*. We ended up talking for nine hours that day and had stayed in close contact ever since. I was the Silas to his apostle Paul, though he always preferred the freedom of obscurity.

Metcalfe walked out of the shack with a cigarette in his hand, his brown derby cap covering his bald head and his oblong glasses obscuring his little eyes. He grinned big with his yellow smoker's teeth and in a voice deeper than I remembered, he asked, "You have trouble finding the place?" I stepped out of the car to give him a hug as Willow walked out wearing a long black dress, black earrings, big black sunglasses, and a huge black hat, looking like *Breakfast at Tiffany's* funeral. She and Metcalfe piled into their car and we went to buy them gas. Once back at the Guidestones we filmed a conversation about their mysterious origins and what they might mean. It was a perfect day. The film producer, Mac Yorkshire, offered me some distilled water he had made himself. "You can't trust what those big companies put in your water, man". His water tasted like a wet dog. After we wrapped everything up I said goodbye to Metcalfe and Willow and headed back to South Carolina. When I got home, Shawn had gotten off work early to spend time with me, so we went to the grocery store to buy stuff for a barbeque. When we got back, we grilled corn and steaks and drank beers. Smiles and laughter abounded and as night came we drank harder and made love till we passed out.

At first light, Shawn whispered in my ear, "I want to take you somewhere special today, baby. You ready for an adventure?" "I sure am, sweetheart". We prepared for a little trip and headed out. I had no idea where we were headed and just enjoyed looking at her, watching her look back at me, smiling, singing songs, and smoking cigarettes. Shawn smoked cigarettes like cigars—only enough to draw the smoke and not inhale. She smoked. I secretly thought this was stupid, but I had plenty of my own foibles to worry about and with a girl this fine, she could have eaten mayonnaise straight from the jar as long as she loved me. After an hour of driving, we came to a fork in the road and stopped for boiled peanuts, Shawn's favorite southern treat. The ruddy grocery store was more like a beat to death vegetable stand, but these kinds of places were the best for finding boiled peanuts. A topless man in his early sixties stood with long, stringy grey hair and big bushy white beard, his ass crack showing a good two inches on his sagged pants: "Yousbedwatchosefthundastoamsgoncomesoon" he said pointing at the sky. We took it that there was an approaching thunderstorm, so we thanked the man for his caution and carried on for another half an hour on the lonely road down into a state park. We came to a parking lot on a hill that led further down to an unknown destination. As we got out, Shawn asked if I was ready. "Yeah, let's go". We walked down a long trail, holding hands and enjoying the wild and raw beauty of the southern woods. "We need to get a big piece of land like this so we can make love in the woods! I'd be your little kitten and you would be my handsome professor". When Shawn put ideas like that into my head, I swooned with lust, not just for her body, but for love.

The pathway began to open up and I heard the sound of running water and walked to a ridge to pee. I could see a river down below me to my right. As Shawn walked down into the opening of river rocks, a swirl of yellow butterflies swept around her like a tornado. It was like watching something out of a movie—the girl walks out into the light and raises her hands in ecstatic freedom as the butterflies swirl—but it was actually happening. I walked down to the river rocks and held her in my arms kissing her deeply. She posed for me in a couple snapshots and we skipped rocks along the water. Little tide pools along the Chattahoochee river held the eggs of frogs and we marveled at the sight. In the distance, we could see dark clouds approaching, so we decided to make our way back to

Tears Like Flowing Streams

the car. As we drove away, Shawn offered another adventure and I agreed to go for it. Twenty minutes down the road we turned onto a smaller road, down into a ravine to another parking lot. "This cave was made in the Civil War and they cut it straight through the mountain, but the war was over before they could finish it, so it goes three-quarters of the way into the heart of this mountain". I walked in with Shawn and the cold, dank spook of the place overwhelmed the senses. I went ahead and began to walk, avoiding any fear that might have been gripping me.

Deeper and deeper we walked until the light of the cave entrance became as small as my thumbnail. We stopped and looked deeper into what felt like the mouth of cold death. "You've brought me to a magical place, Shawn. I'd like to take a moment alone". She started walking back out of the cave and I crouched down and put my palm to the ground, feeling the cold wet stone and letting the breath of the cave blow over me. In the stillness, I closed my eyes, allowing my fear, hope, anger, frustration, hurt, and love to coalesce into one point in my palm. I gave it all to the mountain and opened up my heart to the grim cold that surrounded me. I let myself die in there, if only for a moment. This was my magic.

We returned to Shawn's house. Angie had bought the little girls some new bows and headbands and they were having a make-up party. Shawn decided that she wanted to give me cornrows, since I was in the dirty South, so I let her. While Shawn did my cornrows, Sadie took lipstick and rubbed it on my lips, as carefully as a child possibly could. Sadie giggled with joy at the sight of a bearded man wearing lipstick. After my cornrows were complete, Shawn painted my eyes for the girls and they all laughed. "He must love you, Shawn if he lets you do that to him!" Angie said as she sent the kids off to bed. I looked up at Shawn as she wrapped her arms around me. "I do love you, Shawn"; she looked at me with her big eyes and smiled that childlike smile of hers.

"I have a surprise for you. Just go sit down on the bed". She ran into the kitchen and poured me a glass of whiskey and brought it back, "I need ten minutes. You finish that glass and come see me in the bathroom when it's gone". I sat on the edge of the bed, sipping my whiskey with my freshly done cornrows, pondering what kind of wildness was waiting for me in that room. I got up and walked into the bathroom where the shower was running and candles lit the room. The shower was a large walk-in and there was a tile bench at one length of the shower. Shawn stood like Venus under the shower with her jet black locks streaming down over her tattooed body; the flowers, skulls, and symbols all glistened in the candlelit reflections.

As she stood there under the streaming water I entered the shower and sat down with my head up to her sacred place and began to kiss. She pulled at my head full of cornrows, "It's shark week down

Tears Like Flowing Streams

there, baby". "I don't care", I replied, and resumed my mission. I could taste the blood and water as it streamed into my mouth like I was drinking from the pierced side of Christ. It was holy, it was pure, for it was the essence of my goddess, the blood of my love. When I had satisfied her, she returned the favor and we made love in the water. We lay there, spent under the heat of the room and the thick mist that had formed. We were there together in another world. We returned to the bedroom and played with Murderface together, laughing and drinking more whiskey. There were flashes of light in the distance and the rumble of thunder; we used the sound as an excuse to fall asleep extra close.

At about four AM the lightning had come closer, and we were both awakened by the crashing. It was terrifying, but also brought us to life. The rain fell in long ribbons with drops the size of dimes and everything dirty was washed away. The air was thick and warm and even at this time of night, it was hot outside. Shawn and I looked at each other in the loom of the thunder and without a word ran outside without any clothes. Lightning struck less than a mile away and the night sky was filled with light, showing the contours of Shawn's body. I grew hard in her hand as we kissed and she bent over for me. The thunder was deafening as our limbs slid like serpents, one arm over the other, drenched and barely able to see in the massive gush of rain. I picked her up and carried her to the hood of her car where I took her in the flash and the boom of nature's primacy; and in that place I saw my own flash of light. The drops stood in place. The lightning held still like a dead tree and a continuum of light swept before me, inside and out, spilling me inside of her, onto the ground to be swept away in the flood of passion. We both slid to the ground, washed in the blood, washed in the water, soaked in love.

There was no need for a shower so we dried off and went back to sleep. When dawn came, the storm had passed and the sun crept in in magnificent orange and red. My Apache angel glimmered in the rusted light and I sat up to watch the sun and admire her as she slept. This path I had taken away from all that I knew, once again thrust me into situations that were painful, scary, life-threatening, and sublime; my vision from the Goddess that led me down this path reminded me that greatness is in the doing, not in the thinking; that I must be torn in order to grow. And I was torn apart, ripped to shreds, body and soul ragged and fragmented; but every break made me stronger, more capable of standing pain that would snap other men in two. My will had been sculpted like volcanic rock in the fires of every burned bridge. But where was I going? What was I doing? Why was I here in the arms of Shawn, this vision of beauty? I didn't know that answer, but I was thankful. I nodded to the sun as one would acknowledge a friend, and let the morning sweep over me like fresh sheets.

Tears Like Flowing Streams

At that moment, I was at peace. "I've never loved anyone like you before", Shawn said as her eyes fought her waking consciousness. I had known a deep love with Betty and a lighter kind with many other women, but none so fierce and hot as what I felt for Shawn. "Neither have I, Shawn".

Chapter 30

SHAWN HAD TO WORK LIKE CRAZY FOR THE next several days and I had no money, or place to go. Marooned in some small cul-de-sac, miles from the small town, deep in the wet-hot heart of the South, I simply tried to devise my next step. If the big job would not materialize, then perhaps I should try the University of Washington. Maybe they had something for me. I decided that I would return to work with my brother and make a run at graduate school in my hometown. Shawn and I had leveled out and whatever demons she had been hiding were hidden well for the time being. James contacted me and said he needed me to come back to help him with his somber return to Washington. I agreed and let Shawn know. I could see the distance in her eyes as she processed what that meant. She, like many of us, held a deep sadness in a well that was buried, covered, nailed down, and sealed with concrete; and somehow that news fell into the well adding to the poison that stagnated since long before my arrival. But with just two days before my departure and no guarantee of when we might see each other next, we resolved to mock the sadness and party hard.

Sadie and Amber got a slip 'n' slide and I helped Shawn set it up for them. I blew up a big, inflatable pool and set it in the yard, filling it with cold water. The lawn was inundated with bugs and spiders. You could barely stand on the grass for more than a minute before something crawled over your foot, but the slip 'n' slide and the pool were relatively safe. Whatever ended up there would drown. Nobody could figure out why the slip n slide wasn't slippery, so Angie brought out a bottle of baby oil. Once it was dispersed, it became lightning-fast and the kids slid down and off the end with speed, giggling and screaming like little girls do. Shawn held the bottle of baby oil in her hand and looked at me with a coy smile, mouthing the words, "I want you inside me".

We all got cleaned up and Shawn and I took a long drive, making plans for her to move out to me once I had settled in with school somewhere. I was full of joy at the thought. I imagined myself sitting in a regal leather chair, like the one at the Roosevelt, reading a deep book on the Agora of India; she would be in the other room and would quietly walk toward me in her sun dress. She would gently take the book from my hand and slide off my glasses. "I need some time with my professor", she would say as she lifted her dress and climbed on top of me, and we would make love. At least that's

Tears Like Flowing Streams

how I imagined it would be. Later Shawn took me to her bar and introduced me to everyone, all gentle folk with that gritty bar kind of class. I had worked at a craft beer and whiskey bar in Brooklyn, so it was odd to see the trashy style of drinks promoted. Signs for Alabama slammers and appletini shots littered the walls, but it seemed to fall in line with the general æsthetic of the town.

Shawn took a shot, but I was taking it slow, assuming I would need to drive. Somebody needed to drive us home and after the scare the other night, I genuinely wondered if the whiskey had been affecting my virility, so I refrained. Shawn on the other hand took shot after shot and became a boisterous caricature of herself, tussling her hair big and throwing her hips and shoulders around with "hot sex" written on her lips and eyes. She would dance around in her tight jeans and loose white top to everyone's amusement, smiling and laughing, but I could see the cracks in the veneer and the sadness that fled the light of every smile—she was in mourning.

The night drew to a close, at least at the bar, and I drove the car down the lonesome roads of that lonesome hollow while Shawn blasted Pulp through the car stereo. In the darkness of the misted eve, Shawn opened up the sunroof, took off her top, and stood in the passenger seat, howling and singing, and dropped back down to stick her tongue in my ear. My rock-n-roll queen put her head down in my lap while I drove. All of this had been so surreal, especially for a man whose ego had been crushed. I felt undeserving of anything good and I was being given the sexual feast of kings by my Apache angel.

When we got to her place she threw me onto the bed and took my clothes off, poured whiskey in my mouth, straight from the bottle and said, "I'm going to let you go where no one else has ever gone". She pulled the baby oil out and sprayed it all over both of us and straddled me with her hand now behind herself. And in one movement, she let me in. A look of shock and wild pleasure flashed across her face and I lay still, letting her do what she wanted. I was beyond words as she began to move and throw purple sparks of energy from her body like a blown transformer. And not too long later I saw the white light again—the flow of spirit and soul from mine to hers—and we were spent.

It was the day before I left and she was hungover. We went to a local park and walked around, just holding hands, feeling the breeze and watching the tall grass sway. Whatever passion that we had was matched with a shrouded sadness that collectively held our atmosphere and we tried to slough it off, touch faces, and rain down kisses, but the sadness was there. It was a stern fact that I would again be three thousand miles away and that she would be there in that little southern town, making appletinis for the locals and I would be back home, wherever that was, trying to claw my way back to a respectable existence. But then and there, we were in a kind of shadowed bliss,

Tears Like Flowing Streams

swearing our love for each other and plotting how we would live through separation. It seemed like an uphill climb. Shawn promised me she would fly out in three months after her new management position became stable, and I agreed I could wait for her that long. Nobody was around for acres and acres and she pulled her dress up in the middle of the grassy field and pointed down, "You see this pussy here? This is the best pussy in the world and it's nobody's but yours. I'm saving it for you, so you better respect it!" "I understand. My dick is yours too baby. I'll wait for you".

That night we went out for dinner and I swelled with love for Shawn. I felt like a man who had half of the equation of the good life and would be going home to prove I could find the other half. Shawn was exhausted from the night before and we went to bed early, playing with Murderface and watching a movie. She fell asleep clinging hard to my arm and I didn't want to undo it even though it was painful. I fell asleep too.

I awoke at dawn as the crimson glow opened my eyes. In the morning gloam I lay uncomfortably with Shawn still on my arm. What goodness and grace I had in this world of love would be taken from me; or I should say it would be given away to fate as I tried to clean up the wreckage of my past and build something new for the both of us. We talked in terms of us at all times and our aspirations became the same. She awoke and climbed on top of me, her shining body in the red, vestal light, making love to me once more before she had to say goodbye. I gathered my things, said goodbye to Sadie, Amber, Angie, and Chris, and left with Shawn. The hood of her car was still blood stained from the night we made love in the thunderstorm, and she kept it as a kind of morbid, magical memento. We made it to the gas station where the Greyhound would pick me up for Atlanta and sat staring at each other. The gold of the sun was kissing her skin as she stared at me, too somber to say anything. We kissed again and again and squeezed again and again. This red letter love was as powerful as a punch to the heart and potentially as deadly; this love was my ray of hope. As Shawn drove away, it was like watching a sinking ship where nobody was sure if there would be survivors.

Chapter 31

THE BUS RIDE WAS SOMBER, THE PLANE RIDE was somber; the color of the world had been sucked out and all I had was the emptiness of growing distance. All I wanted was Shawn and she was there being all those things I wanted, and I left because I couldn't give her a half-broken man and expect her to be happy with it. James picked me up when I arrived in Minneapolis and as I began to gab, I realized it wasn't appropriate. He was pale like ghosts had been stealing his soul in the night and the façade of joviality I was holding quickly fell. We were plunged into a similar place. Lovelorn, love lost, lovesick. Catherine and James had planned a divorce party for the next day; I had never heard of such a thing. When we got back to his old house, Catherine was there making snacks and poured me a glass of wine, "so how was your trip, meeting the long lost love of your life?" "Oh, it was great. She was great. I just don't know what the hell I'm going to do to try to get that girl out to me". "Yeah, that sounds tough, but I hope for the best for you".

James left the room to run a quick errand and Catherine came and hugged me, "I'm so thankful that you are here to be with James". She began to weep what seemed like metered tears; ones that, though they came out, would not allow the indignity of becoming too abundant. "Goddammit, I love that man and...this, this is so hard. You boys are just, everything and you charm the world". I wept with her, but not too much. I was trying desperately to be appropriate and caring, but I had plenty of my own sorrow to bleed out in salt water. After the hug, we returned to bullshit conversations about things that don't matter; which were pretty much anything other than love. And though the house was similar in spirit to Chris and Angie's house of divorce, this place still kept its grace and somehow that made a world of difference. This made me keep wondering why the fuck we even do this? Why do we put ourselves in this position of such great potential for destruction? Then I saw the answer in Catherine's face. We do it because we know love is real and if we can somehow overcome our own shit and accept the other's we might be able to find that slow, steady, scarred, gilded broken bowl of love. Sometimes that break shatters into too many pieces, sometimes its left discarded too long, sometimes it was never suitable to hold anything at all other than the idea. I messaged Shawn.

The next day, we spent our time gathering up items for the divorce party and I washed all of my

Tears Like Flowing Streams

clothes. I helped James pack up his things from his old bedroom with Catherine. We folded his suits and shirts and placed them in boxes. Both of us had lost serious weight, James at thirty-five pounds and me at fifty. Divorce is a motherfucking weight loss plan like no other. Shirts that no longer fit James now fit me, so I inherited several very nice dress shirts and blazers. James didn't know what to get rid of and what to keep. Everything made us cry. The ache of a broken bone is about the same as the ache your whole body feels when something so congealed and consummated is broken and there was no relief or escape.

When we were done putting everything in boxes, we went downstairs and helped Catherine prepare for the party, and decided to go to the store. The spirit was of light-hearted jokes on heavy subjects, and each laugh brought a tear. This was respect; this was dignity like I had never seen in my life.

When we got back it was less than an hour before guests would arrive, and I showered and put on my new shirt and blazer with my jeans and dress shoes. I took my time getting ready, because I was a cocktail of emotions. I snapped a selfie to Shawn in hopes that she would remember that her man was handsome and in love with her; this mix of love, lust, and loss was really hard to handle and I reached for a large glass of wine to soften the blow.

As guests arrived, I decided to help keep things light and offered people tarot readings. Nobody objected and so I kept doing them. This allowed me to become friends with everyone in the room and talk about heavy things in other people's lives, but not my own and certainly not Catherine and James'. The air was thick with a sterile kind of love, the kind you feel in a hospital room as a relative passes away in the presence of family. It was beautiful and shameful; not shameful for sins, or slander, but just humble and bruised, like licking open wounds after a thrashing. Catherine never looked so beautiful as she did there in the lull of dim light, the sparkle of glassware, the glinting eyes of strangers; everything reflected to her. And my dear brother James, the one who had changed my diapers and thrown spaghetti at me in my childhood high-chair to "see if it was ready" was there too, slimmed down, handsome, smiling, yet glowing like a punched face. This whole night was a giant bruise whose process of healing was capable of every color. Hands lay on shoulders, tears fell on hands, soft voices swept through the room like the whirring of wheels and I drank wine. When the night was over and everyone had left; we all turned in and I thought of Shawn.

The next day, James and I hit the road after a series of long and aching goodbyes, and though there was hurt all over, it was like surgery had been successful and we were now outpatients. The ride back to Washington seemed half as long as the ride there, and before we knew it we were home.

Tears Like Flowing Streams

Home—now there's a place. What is that place exactly? Is it the door, the furniture, or perhaps the dishes? James and I set out to find out as I helped him pick out his furniture and other household items. He got himself a little place we called "The Turtle House" because of its green color and diminutive size. It was perfect for him in many respects; close to water, close to beer, and not too far from the freeway for work. He paid me to paint the place and it kept me in living money for a while. Money was thin and with nothing but a faint hope of a chance at the University of Washington, I didn't have much going on.

I messaged Shawn all of the time; too much. I wished so bad for her to be with me and I was worried that she would lose interest. Something in the way she reacted to me when I first got to her home scared the shit out of me and jarred something loose. I was drinking more than I wanted to and was hungover every morning. On nights when others didn't drink, I begrudgingly only had one or two. I wanted fucking oblivion, and fast—and a time machine that would take me to that future where Shawn and I could be together and all of my plans for grad school would come true. I couldn't tell if that was a good dream or a grand delusion, but it was annoying the shit out of everyone who loved me.

The outdoor labor days of construction began as James picked up more jobs for both of us to do, and it was during that time that my fear of loss began to take its hold on me. Shawn would message me cryptic things, like, "this is hard" and "what are we even doing?" I would try to find a time to call, but with timezones and conflicting work schedules it was very difficult to speak. When time off would come for her, she would be busy with daily life, or would be so exhausted that making any effort toward anything felt like too much to ask of her. I loved her with a searing love that made it hard to see straight. James grew increasingly annoyed, though he was also empathetic to my situation. "Listen man, she's three thousand miles away, maybe you should at least consider that this might not be the right situation for a person in your position". I knew James was right, but my heart didn't care and I clung to Shawn all the more. It felt like she was slipping through my fingers with less and less communication, messages of annoyance at my words. I began to feel like it was illegal to talk to the one I loved. It felt like a prison.

I had been pen pals with this girl, Riley, that I had met many years before when she was pining for Hank, back when he and Tahoe lived in Seattle. Now Riley had returned from a three-year stint in Germany where she had almost married a German man, but had somehow been rejected. We decided to meet up to chat at a Tacoma spot where her brother worked. When Riley showed up, she looked different; her beer drinking had had the better of her and she wore it a bit, but she was stylish and nice and I wasn't looking to get laid, being so awe-struck and randy for Shawn. I made sure to talk about my girlfriend a lot to keep things clear.

We decided to go back to James' place to cook dinner, and since I was staying with him, it only stood to reason it would be a safe, cheap place to drink and chat. The night pressed on and Riley became a bit more sloppy. I had been drinking a good deal of whiskey, but I always kept a good poker face and the deep conversations continued. James had messaged that he would be home soon and I let him know Riley was there. When James arrived, Riley looked at him like he was an intruder, "Who is this guy?" James replied with a courteous smile, "Why I am the man of the house and you are my honored guest". "Ohhh really?"

I chimed in, trying to stop whatever weird thing was coming to fruition. "Yes, Riley, this is my brother James, the one I told you has been keeping me off the streets. Remember I told you that?" Riley, as if instantly blotto, plopped back down into her chair with her whiskey, "yeah, well he comes in here judging me like the big white man he is", her eyes slid like bubbles over a bathtub until she caught them again. "White man? Aren't you white? What does me being white have to do with you hanging out in my house as my guest?" James replied. "I am of the proud Lakota race, I can speak the language. I can speak German! I can speak Lakota! I can speak Spanish and English! What can you speak Mr. Serious?" James looked at me with his "get this crazy person out of here" eyes. I tried to tend to the conversation, but it devolved into Riley incoherently yelling at us in foreign languages. "Riley, neither of us speak German" "That's right, because you killed the Indians!" "What? Wait, what are you talking...okay, it's time to wrap things up here". I mouthed "I'm so sorry, I have no idea what the fuck just happened" to James as I picked Riley up. She looked up and smiled at me and her head dunked and bobbed like a buoy on choppy waters. "I'm gonna sleep here tonight. Which bed do I sleep in? Not with Mr. Serious there. Where's the bed?" I took her into the guest room where I had been sleeping and laid her down on the bed, taking off her shoes for her. "Wh...what are you doing to me?" "I'm taking off your shoes so you can sleep. I'm going to sleep on the floor, Riley". "Wuh? What the Fughk are you talking about, don't be a pussy, get up here". I wanted to just get her to pass out before James came in and threw her out on the street. I laid down beside her, envisioning Shawn in glowing slow motion in that field, pointing to her lifted skirt, "you see this pussy? It's yours alone". I told Riley I had to get up to pee. When I came back she was still in the bed talking to herself and then to me, "I'm gonna let you have *this*..." She rubbed my hand down to her lady parts, "Riley, I can't...I can't". I pulled my hand back, "I *can't!*" "Wuh, why not? It's good...why don't you wanna?" "Riley, I am in *love* with my girlfriend. I'm only in this bed with you so you'll be safe and stop giving me shit". As if I hadn't said a word, "Oh, *I* get it". Riley looked at me like a proud mother. "You're *gay*, right? Ah, I can see it now". "No, Riley, I'm not gay, I'm just in love with my girlfriend, Shawn. My girlfriend I've been telling you about all night?" "It's okay, I can help you come out! Oh, and we can have a coming out party and you can come live with me!" "No, Riley, I don't think so".

Riley got up and stumbled out of the room. The house was very loud with movements and she thumped like an elephant. The sound of a bottle opening could be heard, then drinking and a twist shut. She lumbered like an ox down to the bathroom, staggered back, and eventually became silent. Then out of nowhere she leaned in and began to kiss my face. I tried to move away, but she kept going. She looked at me in the dark, as if confused about who she was kissing and started to hit me, "I loved you and you didn't want to marry me! Why didn't you want to marry me!" She had told me about her German boyfriend and how they were engaged and somehow he lost interest, but judging by the situation I was in, I got a better idea of why this had happened. I calmed her down and she finally fell asleep. I slid quietly down onto the floor and slept there till morning.

When dawn came, James poked his head in the door, "Get that crazy bitch out of here". He said with his serious smile. "I will, I'm gonna take her to her friend's house". When Riley woke up I hustled her out the door and drove her to her friends. "We should get together again sometime soon!" "Yeah, I'll meet with you over *coffee*". I said with a smile. Later that day she blocked me on social media.

Chapter 32

NOT LONG AFTER, SHAWN MESSAGED ME: "Why would you tell me you were out with a girl? What are you trying to say? Listen if you want to go fuck every little hussy that walks your way, go ahead!" "What!? No! I told you so you wouldn't worry, just like when you do". "You mean like when I told you about Nevada Randy? He's like my brother! I would never say something like that to you!" "Wait, what, baby you've misunderstood me. I love you!" "I'm not stupid, I know what you were trying to do". "No, baby, no…" Shawn hung up. The irony of turning Riley down for sex the night before was not lost. It felt like it didn't even matter, like it was some kind of amorous joke that I should find this girl and be swept from her like a mouse in a pastry shop. We talked the next day and she seemed to understand that my intentions were good, but she had a jealous streak and a possessiveness that worried me as the weeks went by. I sent her an email:

I have insomnia. I'm thinking about you and me and how awesome it will be to wake up next to you and enjoy your beauty, your eyes as they first open in the morning. My dreams are simple. I daydream about cooking you dinner and walking along the water. I dream about the day we set foot in our little house in our own little piece of property. I dream about making love that takes us to new heights of vision and passion. I long to sing with you and pass endless days with songs, dancing, wine, and good company. Every moment since you and I began, my mind takes me to a safe place where it is you and me. Every day I work towards that goal and all the others that complement our bright future. I belong to you and adore you. This little love note will help me sleep. I'll call you when I wake up. I really would love to see your face. xoxo!

The next day, Shawn told me I couldn't message her so much, so I tried to back it off, but all that did was make me feel anxious that she wouldn't know how I felt, that I was making personal progress. I told her I had confronted a family member about a longstanding issue with verbal abuse I needed to address. I told her my sister thought I was a thief because she had been robbed and thought I had done it. I told her that I had applied to get into the University of Washington and that I was doing everything I could to grow something new and wonderful in my life. I told her my books were selling well. I told her anything I could to keep her in the loop, but from her I heard virtual silence.

Then the day came when she said nothing at all and I tried not to message her, but couldn't help it. I asked if everything was okay. Nothing. I offered a plan to come see her. Nothing. Not long before we had spoken every night on video and laughed and joked and planned, but that was all before my visit. Now that she had a new schedule she could never do that. She could never call, she could never message; I was in love with a name and a picture on a computer screen. Night came and I somehow missed her call. There was a voicemail; the voice was soft, somber, and gritty like Shawn's, but it was further than three thousand miles away.

"Hey, I'm sorry I haven't responded today. I... I don't know what to say to you. I don't know if I can keep doing this. We're both trying to live our lives separately, and it's just too intense. I can't handle it. I think you know this is true and it's been coming for a while now. Call me when you get this".

James had a bottle of bad-tasting whiskey and I opened it up and took a big swig. I had bought a six pack of beer and used it to wash the whiskey down. After about three big pulls and a beer, I was ready to call Shawn back. The phone rang and she answered and my voice trembled as I spoke.

"I...I understand, Shawn. I've tried so hard to show you who I am and what I will do, but I'm afraid you have no proof of my former successes, no evidence to back up my promises. I can't help but want to talk to you, but I feel like I'm not allowed to. I feel like the one thing in all this world I love the most is the one thing I can't reach out to. I know this makes me seem crazy and desperate. James has told me I'm behaving like I'm manic and I agree". I took another large pull of whiskey. "I'm sorry I don't have any money, I can't buy your way here, and I can't take care of you".

Shawn with stern love in her voice replied: "It's too much pressure. You tell me these wonderful things and I just can't go crazy for you because it's not safe. It's not safe and I have plans. I want to be a singer, that's going to be my career, that's what I'm going to do for me. I want to go to Peru. I have plans and you need to take care of yourself". I wanted to scream, "I am! I am! I am kicking ass every day!" But I didn't, because in the end, if she didn't see, she would never see. We hung up and I slumped down onto the floor and screamed her name at the top of my lungs with tears gushing, *"Shaaawn! Shaaawn! Fuuuck!"* I pulled a quarter of the bottle of whiskey down in gagging swigs and nearly wretched on the floor. I wrote her an email:

"One day the world will know how much I have loved you. It will make us timeless. It will make us immortal. But more than that it will bond me to you, which is all I ever wanted. You and I in the love we really wanted in our heart of hearts. The love that worked".

Tears Like Flowing Streams

I washed it down with the beer. I sat kneeling like a child at prayer and drank and cried like my whole family had died. I wept and tore my clothes and the booze spilled all over me. I drank the beer to wash the booze and after hours of weeping and drinking, the whiskey was empty and the beer had spilled into a puddle on the floor, mingling with my tears. No matter how hard I drank, my heart was pulled out of me like a bandage yanking hair, and I wanted to die.

It was then in that moment that I lamented every woman I ever hurt, everyone whose heart I had broken. I mourned for my arrogance and my selfishness, I mourned for my heart and theirs. I was crushed under the weight of love's dark comedown and it hit me like I had never felt in my life. That white-hot love burnt me the blackest and I was undone completely. I awoke in a pool of tears and spilled beer to the sound of James washing dishes in the kitchen.

I walked into the kitchen looking like death warmed over, and as soon as my eyes met James', I burst into tears. James stopped washing and came and held me up with his hug and petted my head, holding me tighter than he ever had in our lives. "It's okay baby boy…it's okay…I'm here…your big brother is here". James walked me to his couch so I could sit down. I was shaking with red eyes, glazed with booze and tears, and I was trembling like my car had been struck. James brought me into the guest room and tucked me in. "I want you to stay here until tomorrow. I'll bring you water if you need water. I'll bring you food if you need food". I just wept and wept until I fell asleep again.

I slept until two the next day and felt like someone had scooped out my guts and left a red balloon inside that just floated in the void. I felt neither good, nor bad, just the raging glow of complete and total loss. "Get dressed, we're going out", James said as he popped his head in the door. I put on my clothes and walked out like a hospital patient, and followed him to his truck.

We went down to the waterfront near the University of Washington's Tacoma campus, in front of the Museum of Glass. It was night and the lights behind the sculptures sent colors through the night.

"You and I are very similar, we give our love to everyone like we are buying lottery tickets, hoping to win. We buy as many tickets as we can afford until we are broke and have nothing to give. I think we need to be more like love philanthropists—people who give out our love from abundance. We don't give everything away so we have nothing for ourselves, but we give it to the people who show they could use our love and will reciprocate. We need to be love philanthropists". I was still numb with shock. James continued: "You know, you've given this girl everything you had, but what did she give you back? She didn't earn what you gave her. It's like you mistook her good looks and hippie talk for the real thing, but she never really demonstrated any of that. From everything I've seen, she didn't deserve what you gave her". These words hit me hard. I had been desperate to share love and gave everything I had, but got nothing in return.

*The king uses this
to march out.
There are honours.
He executes the chief,
the captives are good.
Not a mistake.*

I CHING, HEXAGRAM 30, LINE 6

Chapter 33

FOR THE NEXT COUPLE OF MONTHS I FOCUSED on working and trying to get into school. I wrote Shawn a letter I would never know she received and tried to let her go with the sealing of that letter. New opportunities arose and I was invited to speak at a symposium in Joshua Tree in September. I gladly agreed and found myself on several national radio shows talking about my book on consciousness. I had been drinking a lot and was hungover almost every day. No matter what I did, I could not get Shawn off my mind and I lamented her in waves. I had been living between the family house out on the peninsula and James' place in Tacoma.

While I was out at the peninsula house, I went down by the water and read the *Tibetan Book of the Dead*. Within its pages, I found the rites that are given to those who have passed away. The descriptions of what the spirit must do after passing made me think directly of the little death I had experienced in the loss of this white-hot love.

I read these words:

> At this time his relatives are crying and weeping, his share of food is stopped, his clothes are removed, his bed is taken to pieces and so on. He can see them, but they cannot see him, and he can hear them calling him, but they cannot hear him calling them, so he goes away in despair. He will grow faint with fear, terror and bewilderment, so at this moment the great showing of the bardo of dharmata should be read. Calling the dead person by name, one should say these words very distinctly:

> "Oh child of noble family, now what is called death has arrived. You are not alone in leaving this world, it happens to everyone, so do not feel desire and yearning, you cannot stay, you can only wander in samsara. Do not desire, do not yearn...Oh child of noble family, whatever terrifying projections appear in the bardo of the dharmata, do not forget these words, but go forth remembering their meaning:

> Now when the bardo of dharmata dawns upon me, I will abandon all thoughts of fear and terror, I will recognize whatever appears as my projection and know it to be a vision of the bardo; now that I have reached this crucial point I will not fear the peaceful and wrathful ones, my own projections.

The King Marches Out

A great roar of thunder will come from within the light, the natural sound of dharmata, like a thousand thunderclaps simultaneously. This is the natural sound of your own dharmata, so do not be afraid or bewildered. You have what is called a mental body of unconscious tendencies, you have no physical body of flesh and blood, so whatever sounds, colors and rays of light occur, they cannot hurt you and you cannot die. It is enough to simply recognize them as your own projections. Know this to be the bardo state".

It was in the reading of these words that I realized I must be dead to Shawn, to be as dead, neither able to speak to or touch her; that I must move on lest I become what the Tibetans call a "Hungry Ghost", doomed to hunger for a kind of human connection that would never materialize. For the alcoholic, the desire would always be there, but no drink would ever sate, for the lover, no connection could be felt. It was this death I experienced, this loss of white-hot love that had driven me to the edge of sanity as I fought for my own soul. I had grown faint with fear, terror, and bewilderment, and I had to move on. My dreams and visions of Shawn were illusions, my own projections, and when I recognized this, they held power over me no longer. But Shawn wasn't the only mortal vice possessing me. I was beholden to the power of alcohol; to numb the pain of existence, to celebrate and to mourn, but everything had become numb. Whether in joy or pain, I was always numb, neurotic, and trembling in the chaos of being.

I read a book called *Turning your Mind into an Ally* by Sakyong Mipham. In it he spoke of how our hopes and fears are two sides of the same coin, robbing us of the present moment. These words hit me hard, because it seemed that all of my life was occupied by some distant future in which I would find that elusive prophesied greatness; that at some point, all would be perfect, the golden sun of my joy would shine endless in resplendent rays of satisfaction in the arms of my faceless love. All this time I was numbing the moments away with the sweet taste of Johnnie Walker Black and cheap red wine, gliding the lonely skies of Bacchus in a holding pattern, waiting to land upon greatness like a triumphant bird of prey. The thought golem, made of every dissenting voice that arched over me like an army of bardo demons clanked and scratched its rusted claws along the soft walls of my stillness. It was my hungry ghost, my most secret companion and my mortal enemy.

I was alone at my parents' place and was very lonely, but the words of Sakyong Mipham were marching like an army toward my thought golem and there would be a confrontation in the red flood of wine. The drink tasted sour and so I drank more to kill the taste; the bottle of red wine was empty. I sat in my room and tried to just lay there in stillness, but the golem knew his kingdom in the caverns of my mind was in jeopardy and he would not let me go. My loneliness was crushing me, telling me what a piece of shit I was, that I had failed my children, that I had failed my marriages and that I would fail at getting my life back in order. I would never know peace and I would always be a fucking piece of shit that people secretly reviled. I was thought a thief, a loser, a druggie, a drunk, a deadbeat, a lost cause, a moron, and a total waste of skin. I walked to the bar in the game room, reached for the unopened bottle of Tito's vodka, unscrewed it and looked in the mirror as the thin, hollow soul of a man looked back at me, starved in a desert of his own making and howling like a hungry ghost.

"I'm an alcoholic".

Chapter 34

I TOOK A LONG HARD PULL ON THAT BOTTLE of vodka, gagging down an eighth of it, wincing as the warm, uneasy agent of my glory and grief washed over my golem, bathing him in the sweet-hot nectar of my failure and shame. I carefully placed the bottle back on the shelf and walked to my bed. I turned out the lights and watched the golem swim round my thoughts, spitting and cursing the utter folly of my existence. When I woke up, I decided I was done drinking.

Day after day came and I refrained from offers to drink. I spent my time building things with James and trying to be present, not allowing the golem his prized meals of fear and hope. I watched with sadistic pride as he starved because every day that I didn't drink was a day that he lost. It was a little life where I had experienced so many little deaths. I wrote to Robert, who had so graciously helped me when Hank threw me out on Skid Row on Valentine's day:

Sup bro? Been thinking a lot about you. I'm taking a crack at sobriety. I'm four days sober. I've developed a neurosis and fear that stems from my long term drinking habits and though I've cut back I feel I need to just let it go. I know you've known I'm an alcoholic for a long time and so have I. I have the support I need here. It's fairly easy for me to refrain and I know why I have imbibed more often than not. Mostly to feed the beast in my mind, to sing it to sleep with the voice of Johnnie Walker and turn its cry to a coo with rich red wine. But I want to feel. I want to feel the discomfort of existence and meditate instead of medicate. Perhaps one day I can have a healthy relationship to alcohol, but for here and now it is a mental and physical stumbling block. I'm telling you because I know when I tell you I'm serious. I'm serious. I'm happy to finally live in my own skin and be okay without a girl or a drug or a drink or any other influence to occupy me and my monster. Now that I've identified this parasite in my mind I'm spending my time meditating it into starvation. I love you.

Robert: That's really great news, man, I've been there as you know and the first step of realizing I needed or wanted change was the hardest one. If there is anything I can do to help or support you please let me know. I love you and believe in you. xoxo

The King Marches Out

Gabe: Thanks bro. Its all part of the great work I've been going on. I love you too! I'm so thankful to have you in my life.

Robert: Of course, anything for you. We can talk anytime about this stuff I know it can be hard at first. Are you going to do any work on the drinking issue specifically? Meaning get into the root of it, if that makes sense?

Gabe: The root is the need to feel completed, satiated. It comes from being convinced at childhood that I was incomplete; that I was in need of something outside. It is the consumer mind that uses all things. We can talk soon.

I felt a sense of victory over the monster of inadequacy that had plagued me since I was little; that voice that tells you that you are imperfect and in need of an outside source to complete you. I knew that was a vicious lie, I now knew that I was indeed whole and pure in my eternal process of transformation. The perfected Buddha Nature was within me and all I needed to do was to draw from that deep well of infinite compassion and remember the projections of my own which stood themselves up as fierce foes. As the demon armies let loose waves of flaming arrows from their clawed hands, these missiles of illusion transformed to floating blossoms. I was no longer the sorry, starved, sexless, hopeless man in crisis that I was when I left Betty, but finally a man who had taken the chance to venture into the desert of his own existence and return truly transformed. I had somehow found a form of enlightenment from the gutter of existence.

Chapter 35

A FEW WEEKS HAD PASSED AND MY OLD PAL, Zeb, was organizing staff for an annual music festival that happened on Capitol Hill and he asked me to be his right-hand man. The money was good and I decided it would be nice to take in the shows and see the pretty girls rock out. When the time came, I met with Zeb at a café on Pike street at six AM. and he gave me instructions on what we would be doing. "Basically, I need you to be anything I need you to be. If an artist needs water, you are the water boy. If somebody vomits on a doorway, you will be the vomit guy. If there's a security problem, you are security staff. Make sense?" "Yeah". "Okay, cool. I gotta go handle some shit. See those two women with all those signs? The one with the green glasses is Ren and the other one is Liv. They are the signage people and they are going to need your help for the next couple of hours. I'll see you later". "Cool".

I walked over to the ladies who were organizing signs and introduced myself to them. As soon as I had a look at Ren, I was interested in her. She spoke with a soft, smooth voice that made everything seem okay. She could have told me she ate a baby for breakfast and I might have just nodded in soothed agreement. The other girl scampered off to carry out her duties and I was supposed to help, so I followed Ren around like a puppy, asking where I should put signs up. I kept trying to find excuses to be around her, because I knew she was a total weirdo and it was intoxicating.

After I had spent hours putting up "no smoking" signs all over the event space, which had a six-block radius, and just as I put up the last sign, Zeb came up to me: "Why the fuck are there 'no smoking' signs everywhere? These are public streets; we can't stop people from smoking here. Those signs only go in the designated areas where alcohol is served. Who told you to put these up?" "Uhhh, Ren told me". "Yeah, okay, well you can start taking these down. I'll find Ren and let her know where the signs go".

Zeb enjoyed being the boss because it allowed him to really exude his full powers of being a dick. Things were so busy that he had to constantly tell people what to do and since he had about fifty people under his orders, he had no time for small talk. When Zeb found Ren, he lit a cigarette in front of her and said, "you see what I'm doing? I'm enjoying this delicious cigarette. You know why?

The King Marches Out

Because I can and so can anybody else. 'No Smoking' signs only go in the areas where alcohol is served". When I found Ren again, she looked all sheepish and red-faced, her big glasses hiding her startling eyes. "So, I guess we were only supposed to put 'No Smoking' signs up at the bar areas". "Yeah, Zeb told me". "Sorry about that".

We spent the next hour cutting down the signs that were improperly posted and setting up new ones in proper places. When I was done with the task, we lost track of each other in the course of other items that needed our attention. Everything came together smoothly, and the crowds began to fill the six square city blocks in the mid-summer sun. Somehow I had ended up on garbage patrol and spent much of my time milling around, looking for garbage bins to empty. Some asshole had overfilled one of the big rolling containers that moved by tilting it on the back two wheels, so garbage juice spilled all over my arms as I wrestled the bin through the show going crowds.

Through the fence, I heard a voice call my name. "Is that you, Gabriel D. Roberts? *Hey*, it *is* you! I'd recognize that white beard anywhere!" I was covered in garbage juice. "I'm a huge fan of your writing; can I shake your hand, man?" "Awww, I would, but I'm hauling this huge tub of garbage!" "Oh yeah". He looked all star struck. "Of course, man! Well, I'll see you on the internet!" As I rolled the garbage to the big dump trucks, I laughed at myself. Wasn't that every writer's dream, to be recognized in public by a fan? It was nice to have a random person I had never met come greet me out of the blue, but I enjoyed the irony of it happening while I performed janitorial services as everyone else around me partied.

Evening came and the crowds swelled to capacity; a sea of drunk hipsters, rockers, prom-dressed club girls, and all other sorts of human hilarity rubbed nuts to butts as they crowded in for their favorite artists. I realized that none of this appealed to me anymore, not the drunk girls, or the cheap beer, or the allure of being cool; nothing looked the same to me. This was the epicenter of my old stomping grounds; some of my old pals were still working security. Paul was at the Pabst Stage and Gash was over by the Cha Cha entrance; the appeal of it was lost on me. After all, what was I going to find there, but another drunk girl trying to sound profound, or some kid in a Misfits shirt who didn't know who Danzig was? All of it seemed like a small part of a much bigger machine of distraction. Maybe I was being too harsh, but none of it was really all that fun, it was just a time and a place to snap party photos and try to get laid by the same girls our pals had gotten laid with. This wasn't a festival; it was a goddam cesspool. That's not to say there weren't some great bands playing and some good people between the garbage and the spray-tan. I was also quite happy that Hawaiian shirts had come back into fashion.

The King Marches Out

On the second day of the three-day event, I bumped into Ren again. She was sitting on a curb in a bright, floral-colored dress, her knees scraped like a kid that had fallen off a bike. Ren saw me walking to her and looked unflinchingly at me like a koala looks at eucalyptus leaves. I sat down beside her as she held a small green object in her dirty hands. "Do you think this is made of glass, or stone?" I smiled at her with surprise at her odd question. "I don't know". "Put it in your mouth and find out". She handed me the object and I put it in my mouth and it tasted like stone. "There, that's how you know". I tried not to think about the fact that she had picked this little rock up off one of the filthiest streets in Seattle. Ren asked me to join her as she went to visit her friend, who had a place in the apartments next to the Cha Cha, so I followed her there. Once we got inside, Ren disappeared for a moment and emerged with a glass of water, "here you go". I had made everyone uneasy because I was wearing an event staff shirt and they thought I was going to bust them for drinking or something, but I reassured them that I was off-duty and didn't care anyway. Ren stayed busy talking to other people and occasionally popped over to me, but seemed a bit nervous to engage in conversation with me, so after a while I just left. When the last day of the event came, I looked for her all over, but never found her again. I wanted to see her, because she had intrigued me with her reserved, soft, but witchy vibe.

Just as I got off, I asked Zeb if he would see Ren again soon and he said yes, so I asked him to get her number for me and make sure it was okay to call. The next day, Zeb and I went out for lunch. "So, I wanted to talk to you about something. I talked to Ren. She didn't want to give you her number". I was totally bummed out at the news and turned my head down and away in disappointment. "Juuust kidding! She totally blushed and got all 'aww shucks' on me when I mentioned you; here you go, you smooth bastard". As soon as I got her number, I put it in my phone, which had now been turned on under a pay-as-you-go service, and sent Ren a message. I asked if I could see her soon and she invited me over the next day.

When I arrived at Ren's place down by the University District, she invited me in. Her hair was a short bob style like Natalie Portman's in the film, *The Professional*. She was wearing cut-off shorts and some cheap flats, and her large green glasses hid her big eyes that seemed to defy description. Sometimes when I looked into them, they were grey, and other times they were light brown or green. "I was wondering if you could help me with something; my roommates put out a rat trap and killed one and now it's just laying there, dead. I wanted to bury it. Would you like to help me?" Now to a normal man, this would be an odd request, and it was odd no matter what, but what she asked was noble and pure and I had no problem with helping her, so I agreed. We carefully loosed

The King Marches Out

the rat from the trap that had broken its back and placed its body on a shovel. I followed Ren down the stairs to the back yard, which was situated down the slope of the hill, and we found a suitable place in the grass to bury the rat.

I dug the little grave and Ren gathered some flowers for our little friend. Even though he was a rat and was morbidly snapped in half, he was still very adorable and we felt compassion for him. Ren put him in a rag and we placed the morning glories between his paws like a person, closed the rag, and lay his body into the grave I had dug. I carefully put the soil over the rat in his final resting place and placed a brick ornately at the head of his grave with another morning glory laid upon it. "I'm a former minister, Ren. Would you like it if I said a few words?" "Oh, that would be wonderful". I began my eulogy:

Dear rat friend,
You foraged and rooted
through the waste of our human error.
You swept the streets clean for us,
doing your duty as a creature.
We are sorry that Ren's roommates
killed you with their trap,
breaking your back and undoubtedly
forcing you to slowly suffer.
But your suffering is over and you are in that
big cheese shop in the sky;
We acknowledge the value and beauty of your
life, dear friend,

And we wish that you might rest in peace.
Amen

Ren looked at me with an elated gaze. I had done right by her. She offered to go for a walk with me to the arboretum, a long, forested walking park that sat between her house and Lake Washington. We talked without end, finding one thing after the next in common. She told me that she liked to do mixed media art and sold her stuff at the Fremont Market. She hated that so many good things went to waste, things that could be reused and repurposed. I admired her passion for utilizing these kinds of things in her art. As we walked along, we saw a huge piece of birch bark sitting on the ground, a good arm's length worth. We took it with us for Ren to use later in her art.

After hanging out for a couple of hours, she told me her friend was going to meet us, so we met her at a local French café. I bought Ren pastries and coffee and we chatted while we waited for her friend, Nicole. When she arrived she gave me a once over, as if she were seeing if I was fit to be on a date with Ren. She seemed to approve and sat down to chat with Ren and I. After a while, we all got peckish, so we went and got fixings for a giant salad and headed back to Ren's. Once we made it there, Ren realized that she had forgotten her birch bark at the café and lamented its loss. I said my goodbyes to Ren and Nicole and started up the R6. I rode down to the café and put the birch bark under my arm, returning to Ren's to drop it off. I

The King Marches Out

revved my engine and Ren emerged with sheepish happiness at the sight of the birch bark and me. I walked up to her on the stairs and handed the bark to her, and she gave me a big kiss and a hug. I rode away from my first date with Ren, feeling like a hero. I had buried a rat, charmed and impressed her friend, and saved her lost tree bark. I was feeling good.

Where every other woman in my history was a made up of smoke and mirrors, personal projections, rocks songs and poses, Ren was real. She clearly meant what she said and did so with a terse and humorously morbid sense of duty. She was beautiful, not just in the traditional sense of the word, but down to the core of her person. She shared my childlike nature and wanderlust and, like me, was just as apt to play in the dirt as she was to have a fancy business meeting. I had never felt so immediately at ease and without worry about my own smoke and mirrors, in fact those needed to be shed because I saw in her reflection how ridiculous they were. I didn't need to prance like a peacock to win her, I just had to be myself and this was a relief. Perhaps I needed to be broken completely and healed in order to be able to match the realness that Ren so readily shared with me. Perhaps I needed to really be whole on my own before I could contend with a woman who was so natural and true.

Chapter 36

REN AND I CONTINUED DATING AND I WAS enamored by her earthy wisdom, disdain for pretense, and love of nature. In many ways she embodied the ethical views that I had amassed over the few years prior. When she spoke, she spoke truth and she rarely wasted words, which was nice for a guy who has the gift of gab. Though she was so petite, she had a magnanimous gentleness that exuded from her like crystalline rainbow light. It was when I was not looking or expecting anyone that she found me. Our mutual love of magic and synchronicity made it easy to share thoughts and ideas in a flow of phrases that slipped so softly between us. It didn't take long for me to be totally enamored with Ren as she and I grew in grace and love to a steady beat; where so many other women in my past were a facsimile of truth, Ren was my gospel. I used to fall in love with women, but with Ren I simply floated. My application to the University of Washington was submitted and all I could do was wait, so I spent my time working with James and planning the road trip to Joshua Tree with Ren.

I was quite excited about this symposium, not only because I was a featured speaker, but because I would be hosting a conversation with two of my literary heroes, Rupert Sheldrake and Graham Hancock. We would be discussing the problems faced within scientific research regarding mechanistic materialism and its aversion to anything that didn't follow the positivist hardline, leaving no room for spirituality, Jungian synchronicity, or the existence of anything other than this biological existence that could be measured with scales, charts, and microscopes. This was a great benchmark in my career, and I was very excited to be a part of this monumental event.

Ren and I packed up her little white car and brought along her new kitten for good measure—because nothing says "road trip hijinx" like having a ferocious kitten on the road with you for two weeks. James took his motorcycle down and simply planned to meet us there. We decided to go easy on our first travel day and just get to Portland where we would stay with King Louis and Gypsy for the night. When we made it there, King Louis greeted us at the door and let us in. He lit up a bong and gave Ren a hit, but I refrained, not being keen on the way weed makes me feel. I had brought along some non-alcoholic beer so that I wouldn't feel like a stick in the mud while others drank and we caught up on things. Ren wasn't

The King Marches Out

much of a drinker, so my decision to not drink didn't cramp her style. Gypsy came home from work and we discussed the odd nature of experience with DMT, and King Louis gave me some for the trip. "Would you like some mushrooms too? I have some really great ones, enough for you and Ren to have the Terence McKenna strength trip". Ren and I got excited and said yes. Ren's little orange kitten, Paprika, played maliciously with King Louis' dog, Cooter, and we watched as the two did the dance of cats and dogs. We turned in for the night and in the morning, Gypsy and King Louis sent us off with some weed and other goodies. From there we made our way to Sacramento where we stayed with Ren's dad and step-mother.

When we arrived at Sacramento, I did the initial "boyfriend meets the dad" dance and enjoyed the pleasant company of her family. Ren's stepmom gave us some snacks for the road and we headed to LA.

I called up Robert and asked if we could stay the night with him. He said yes, so we made our way to Venice beach and settled in at his place. He took us out to dinner that night at the same Mexican restaurant I had eaten with him before. It had been six months since last I saw him, when Hank had thrown me out on the streets of DTLA, and he was happy to see me back in LA under victorious circumstances. "I'm so proud of you man, this symposium sounds awesome, you got this kick-ass lady with you. I couldn't be more excited!

What's the news with grad school?" "I just found out while on the road, I've been accepted. I'm over the moon! I mean, you know this is half the reason why I set out on this journey". "I know, man. You stuck with it and now you got your shot for that next level. Hardcore, man". After dinner, we settled in for the night.

The next day, we planned to meet up with Ren's friend in Burbank where Paprika the kitten would stay while we were in the desert, so with time to kill we went out to Venice beach. I was all grumpy because we brought the kitten to the beach and it seemed like a hassle to haul him around everywhere, but I chilled out when I remembered that last time I had been at Venice Beach, I was lying like a hobo on one of the distant benches without money, or rest. It's funny how perspective can do that kind of thing to you; I mean, six months prior I was a shipwrecked fool, dirty and dumped into Skid Row, dragged on a lark out to Venice Beach, and my biggest complaint now was that my adorable girlfriend brought an adorable kitten for the ride. I realized that despite all of these blessings, I still could be an ungrateful dick. I repented of my sins and we dropped Paprika off in Burbank, grabbed some dinner and made our way to Joshua Tree.

The sun was setting as we left Burbank and California didn't disappoint with its smog-laden sunset of rusty reds and oranges, lazy breezes, and the scent of sage in the air. The desert began to open itself up as we drove in the dark, and the

The King Marches Out

highway moved under us like a black river to some starlit heaven. The lights of distant towns and casinos rose and fell, the red eyes of the cars before us merged and swayed with the curves of the road, and as we got closer to our destination, the red eyes grew fewer and fewer until it was just Ren and I on the lonesome midnight highway.

We pulled into the campsite and not a soul was to be seen. I had been so gung-ho to get there that I didn't realize we had made it a day early. Ren just looked at me, thinking more than I wanted to really hear, and I apologized for coaxing her into a rapid arrival. The moon was due to be full in a couple of days and the night sky was illuminated with a breathtaking array of stars in an abundance I hadn't experienced in over a decade. When I lived in Seattle, the sky was often overcast and when I lived in New York, the light pollution drowned out all but the brightest constellations, so here I was awestruck by the angelic choir of light. I set up our tent for the night and we settled in, feeling relieved that we had made it to our destination. We made love and fell asleep in the dead silence of the desert, wrapped around each other like ivy.

I woke up long before Ren and walked around looking for some kind of information about what we should do and where we should go. As she slept, I gazed at her pristine face, full of gratefulness and love. I quietly got dressed and sauntered over to the nearest building and looked inside to find it was empty. I tried one of the doors and it opened. I found a bathroom and washed my face. After much wandering, I returned to Ren, who was still curled up under a blanket, and I kissed her face gently. She squeaked and stretched and looked up sweetly. She extended her arms out and made her hands into fists. *"Coffeeee!"* "Oh, you want some coffee, little creature?" She looked up at me with a fake serious face. "Yesssss!" I chuckled and grabbed my Moka Pot and coffee. I gave her ass a nudge and she put on a dress and light-weight blouse, finally donning a big floppy hat like the kind you see in old hippie pictures from the sixties. We walked barefoot to the building I had snuck into before and setup the coffee on the kitchen stove, trying not to make any mess. Ren stepped into the bathroom and emerged in time for the coffee to be done.

As we were pouring the coffee, a man walked in and we asked him where we were supposed to be. "Oh you must be with the symposium people, right? Yeah, they are on the north side of the facilities. We're doing a photographer's conference". "Cool, thanks man! We'll get out of your hair in a minute". "Oh, no worries, take your time. I'm just going to be doing some prep work before everyone else arrives".

Ren and I made our way to the other side of the series of buildings, which overall took up around twenty or more acres, surrounded by Joshua trees and the open desert. By ten in the morning the sun was already bearing down on us, and shade became the number one priority, so we set up our tent between the tall trees that formed a long row that separated the tent area from the trailer area. The trees were full of beehives, but they were the friendly type, so we paid them no mind. Hidden under the large branches, we found relief from the direct sunlight, and I felt vindicated for showing up early since not long after, the whole place filled up with new arrivals. James pulled up on his motorcycle, looking like he had a bowl of dust dropped on him, and we handed him a bottle of water. "Where are you guys camped out?" "Just over there between the trees". "Cool, I'll setup my shit a little down the way so I don't have to hear your racket and nonsense all the time". "Sounds good man".

Ren and I walked up the hill to the main conference area and encountered a pop-up jewelry shop where the artisan and his apprentice displayed crystals, hand-made earrings, wands, tapestries, incense, Hindu iconography, and rings. Ren was instantly excited to talk with Kali, the apprentice jeweler, but I was too tall for the tent, so I stood outside and chatted up the newly arriving attendees. Ren came out of the sales tent. "I just found out that my birthday is the birthday of the Goddess Kali!" "Woah! She's totally my lady, slaying our illusions in order to bring us closer to enlightenment. Very cool". It had dawned on me that Kali, emanation of Durga/Tara, the goddess had been the one calling me ever since that fateful day in my Queens apartment, and that in her many emanations had been with me all along through this journey. She called me to the desert, and here I was in the literal desert having gone through all other kinds of wilderness.

Chapter 37

REN AND I PREPARED FOR THE OPENING ceremony and made our way up. This was a time of celebration after a solid year of mourning and loss, so I rejoiced at all of the lessons learned, the perseverance that was needed to achieve impossible ends, to take a road I had long been afraid to take, to face the devil's night and make it through, transfigured to a man more capable than ever before to face whatever was ahead. And Ren was there with me to celebrate, sweet and brilliant, unattached to false modalities of success and the worries of credit scores and all the other bullshit people hung their lives on. She sparkled like a diamond in the desert, reflecting whatever color was placed before her, as if through her prism anyone's brightest hue could be seen. To me, she was peace incarnate, a well of serenity, a loving oasis. After the opening ceremony, we decided to go relax in our tent and watch the stars. A couple of our newfound friends gathered and talked with us, and I gave one of them the DMT that King Louis had given me. The gift of seeing a whole other perspective shouldn't be something you charge for, so I just let the gift be passed along. Sure enough, as he returned from his first trip, he sparkled with newfound revelation and an overflow of gratitude.

Ren and I spent much of the night making love and talking about the manifold futures at our feet. We talked about ranches and communes, gardening and permaculture, earth ships and yurts; all the best hippie shit you could think of. After so much hurt, loss, and suffering, her rainbow radiance filled me with such optimism that no matter what, when one is called to a hard path, joy comes in the walking, even if the path destroys all that you were.

The next day, I hosted the main speech with the key speakers, my literary godfathers, Rupert Sheldrake and Graham Hancock. The great hall was packed wall to wall with hundreds of attendees, my brother James and my girlfriend Ren in the crowd. As I spoke with these two great men, I felt the beauty of the moment and thought back to the day I left LA on the R6 with nothing but what my backpack could stow and a desperate hope for a better life, unencumbered by the limitations of the small minded; those choking on the green, guttered money-cock of good credit promises and white picket fences that would sooner drown them in a vortex of fear and hope than grant them what they were sucking for; that sweet, sweet taste of the American dream. I had escaped that macabre,

The King Marches Out

Hollywood, back-alley nightmare. I was present and I didn't drink my way into this, I was fully aware and ready for every question, every idea, and every challenge. As the evening's conversation came to a close, I felt my hermetic journey come to a close as well. It was now my time to return as a magician, making merry in the chaos of whatever was ahead. Ren and I decided to eat the five dried grams of psilocybin mushrooms each and see what kind of party the machine elves had planned for my graduation.

We looked at each other, honoring our time and presence as lovers and trippers, and ate the mushrooms one by one until all ten grams were gone between us. The moon shone bright and full, illuminating the desert entirely. We sat and talked, feeling strange as we began to sense the effects of the mushrooms and a deep desire to make love flooded us. We kissed and held each other, moving with ecstatic vibration, slowly moving back and forth with our legs folded as we sat upright, face to face. Just then, Ren's skin turned blue and she flicked her tongue at me, flashing wild open eyes with a gleaming white glow. Her quiet demeanor gave way to the spirit of Kali, who scratched at my back with her radiant blue fingers, sucked on my skin with bloody tongue, and pulled my head to the side, looking like a beast going for the kill. As I made love to the goddess, rainbows of pentacles flooded the tent and our flesh became one organism, writhing and sliding, cracking and shattering reality in a circular pattern like a bullet through glass. The whole world was in the endless light of her beauty and she had finally come to me as my consort and lover, born to destroy my illusions; born to rule as my teacher and queen. Ren had become the embodiment of that divine feminine power, a love greater than the word mother burned through my existence like a rocket sheds flames as it leaves the earth behind. She had called me and I heeded the call and her love was my reward. When Kali left, my sweet Ren returned and we lay there spent, floating like spirits out of our bodies in rapture and that's when they came; the rest of my friends, my eternal loves and companions from the other side of reality; the machine elves had arrived.

I was evenly between worlds and asked them telepathic questions about why they didn't show themselves to us in our waking reality. My vision turned to one of them forming into a giant door made of blood, boar tusks, teeth, bones, and fleshless muscle, giant lidless eyes everywhere, semen and blue hair like lightening bolts. "Do you think they will want to walk through that door? Do you think the rest of your people would like to see what's on the other side? Eh, motherfucker?" I laughed uncontrollably as they showed me this vision and I understood that what they were was undecipherable to most humans and that some things are best left unknown to those who cannot handle what's behind doors like that. As I laughed, they laughed as well, knowing I understood. They spoke again, like a thousand voices in unison, because all of them were one being and yet they were as individual as we are. "We sent you because we're too big. You're the runt of the litter, the smallest one of us. None of us could fit into that skin tuxedo like you". As they spoke, I saw every human spirit living inside their skin like an ill-fitting tuxedo. All of us are uncomfortable in our own skin because, like an ill fitting tux, it is too small for some, and too loose for others; only for the lucky ones does the flesh fit just right.

I described what I was experiencing to Ren and she listened intently, too tripped to share what she was seeing, but not too tripped to touch and caress me, or my skin tuxedo as I now imagined it. I asked them if Terence McKenna was with them. "Oh yes, he's here, but he's not Terence anymore". Thousands of them formed together in clumps, fractals of unimaginable color, unifying to show Terence's face smiling at me through the shapes of their light bodies. I laughed at the thought of some kind of assimilation in the afterlife and they laughed back at me, mocking my happy tone; they made giant flags pop up out of coral tubes with bright fabrics and colors announcing my greatness in sardonic mockery as they yelled out in an oceanic voice: "Oh, look! It's Mister Psychedelic! Let me stand up on this fuckin' stage and tell you all about these guys here!" They jumped around and stood like evil gnomes smiling in caricature with combed hair, like children in fifties era TV shows. "This guy knows all about them!" They spoke to me in a language I understood and in harsh ways that were shocking, yet funny; the deepest truths in a fart joke.

For a long while, Ren and I just lay there holding hands, talking softly about what we were experiencing, feeling love flow back and forth like the pulses we could feel in each other's hands. Bees gently swept through my mind like joyful little souls the size of pennies; there was no harm, or chance of a sting, just a kind of hive love that crossed between electric shock, orgasm, and the warmth of a hot bath. The taste of honey was on my tongue and I kissed Ren to taste hers. As I drew close to her, I fell inside of her being, no longer confined to the realities of corporeal notions of space and time, and I found my place under her rib cage. There she had fashioned a nest for me, made of owl feathers, the bones of small birds, crisp autumn leaves and thin white sticks. There, beside her heart I curled like a cat in front of a heater. Her love light shone in resplendence and I felt completely whole, in need of nothing, full of all being, full of all life, and full of all that is love. Ren's sweetness was my undoing, because it was naked in its intent, flowing radiantly into my existence, bathing me in golden light. It was her voice that called me to the desert years before; it felt like the shock of déjà vu and was remembered like the lyrics of long forgotten song. It was her, but it was

The King Marches Out

not, she was her and she was the goddess.

When we were ready to move around, Ren and I walked out into the moonlit desert and passed massive Joshua trees that seemed to bow and tremble as we walked by; we laughed at how much more real than real this felt. Neither of us had our glasses on, but if felt like we could see the world better than 20/20. It was around three in the morning and the moon was dead center in the night sky.

It gazed down on our naked bodies, watching us as we marveled at its splendor. Our lunar friend became as a great and glorious eye that reflected the sun's light down to us in the dead of night. And like an unfolding rainbow ladder, the moon spun a web around the globe in a hive structure: the whole of the earth wrapped in the hive of the Gaian mind, and we marveled at the sight. The moon herself transformed into a radiantly blooming lotus flower that slowly unfurled like the bloom of a woman at her lover's touch. And there, standing naked in the moonlight, hand in hand with Ren, I realized that I had met the goddess, made love to her, seen the other side of reality, and had come to a new form of gnosis in which I was no longer the fearful neophyte, but a magician who would navigate the next wave with grace and wisdom. When I started out down that lonely road, to the desert of love, the desert of wealth, the death of all that I knew, I had no idea that the goddess would meet me in the flesh. That resplendent rainbow serpent and the mystery of her voice became clear.

She was a part of me and I was a part of her. The machine elves, the goddess, the dead and the living, were all connected in this hive of consciousness, and it was only a difference of what channel my mind was in to see them all.

The world is full of darkness, shadows, and misery; full of beautiful lies that rob us of the present and suck our youth from us while we sleep awake. There is no knowledge but that which is earned and kept, no knowledge worth keeping that isn't hard won, or earnestly sought. The distance between us all is an illusion; you and I are one and in love, but we must find the barriers that hold us back and keep us from finding a better way together. The hero's journey was complete, but a new journey was beginning to come forth. I had done so many things wrong for so long, justified bad behavior, and I still have so far to go, but enlightenment is not a distant destination on the horizon; it is a constantly changing state of being in which the light flows eternally and releases its peace. It is found where we are, whether on a mountaintop or in the gutter. We are fooled to think there is a real place called, "making it", and we need only look at the celebrities who have lost their money, the bankers who have been found frauds, and the heroes who have failed to see that this life is not about making it, but making love, creating, and learning. Magic is not a means to riches, or a way to fool people into loving you, but a method of navigating life by understanding the road signs, standing up to

The King Marches Out

your fears, and defying the falseness of what our moneyed masters tell us our existence is for. "Be patient, be willing to compromise, be reasonable, be humble", these are the linguistic bricks on the pathway to mediocrity. Burn a fucking hole in your world. Love on fire. Learn like you are starving for each new word, and speak from the authority of the holy mountain; for if you don't, you are robbing yourself of the very legacy you yearn for, and you will never be free. We strive to be perfect in word and deed, but we must remember that no person is "all hero". Enlightenment is not a moment, but an endless series of moments for those who seek it.

What some may see in my life as a series of fuck ups and failures, I see as a series of attempts to free myself from the relentless entanglements of the remaining tendrils of a powerful false paradigm. I am free, but the imprint, the scars, and the histories, remain. Our stories are not over. In all of this, I have learned to allow no shaming authority to surreptitiously take my life and times from me, but instead, dare to live in a way that frightens me. Now I can think of no other way but to live so boldly that it terrifies and inspires those who are so entwined in those old, thorned tendrils that they see apocalypse when they see this life fully realized.

fin

ABOUT THE AUTHOR

GABRIEL D. ROBERTS is a theological scholar, researcher and public speaker specializing in the nature of perception and belief. After twenty-seven years of passionate searching, Roberts stepped away from his long held Christian faith into a more expansive and fluid worldview. The details and reasons are catalogued in his book, *Born Again to Rebirth*. Like many others who have had an earnest thirst for the answers to the big questions of life, Gabriel was not satisfied to settle for not knowing more. His previous book, *The Quest for Gnosis*, explores the roots of belief, the power of the ecstatic state in one's spiritual life, and the means by which a deeply satisfying spiritual life may be achieved outside of the bonds of dogma. Gabriel has interviewed the brightest minds in this field of study, including Dr. Rupert Sheldrake, Graham Hancock, Daniele Bolelli, Peter J. Carroll, Hamilton Morris, Dr. Aaron Cheak, David Metcalfe, Dr. Rick Strassman, and many more.

Gabriel writes for *Vice, Disinfo,* and *Reality Sandwich*, and is the author of four books. He is presently working towards his doctorate at the University of Washington in his hometown of Tacoma (Washington, USA).

www.ingramcontent.com/pod-product-compliance
Lightning Source LLC
Chambersburg PA
CBHW021138080526
44588CB00008B/109